MATHEO ARNESEN

Breaking Free from Living Paycheck to Paycheck

The Ultimate Guide to Financial independence and Wealth Management

To all those who dare to dream of financial independence,
To those who strive tirelessly to break free from the shackles of financial constraints,
To the resilient souls who never give up on their pursuit of abundance and autonomy,
This guide is dedicated to you.

May the wisdom within these pages empower you,
May the insights fuel your determination,
May the journey towards financial freedom be filled with growth, joy, and fulfillment.

Suddenly, it dawns on you: financial freedom isn't measured by the size of your bank account, but by the choices it affords you to live fully

— MATHEO ARNESEN

Contents

Preface

Let me tell you a story about how I finally broke free from the cycle of living paycheck to paycheck and ventured into entrepreneurship. Not too long ago, I was stuck in a rut, working tirelessly to make ends meet with each paycheck barely covering my basic expenses. It was a constant struggle, and the stress was taking a toll on my well-being.

But then, something changed. I decided that enough was enough. I made a commitment to myself to break free from this cycle and create a better life for myself. I started by meticulously budgeting and cutting back on unnecessary expenses. Every dollar saved went towards building an emergency fund, slowly but steadily creating a safety net for myself.

As I gained more control over my finances, I began exploring opportunities to increase my income. That's when I stumbled upon a unique idea— a laser engraving business. I've always had a passion for crafting and creating, and laser engraving seemed like the perfect blend of artistry and entrepreneurship.

I took a leap of faith and invested my savings into purchasing a laser engraving machine. With determination and hard work, I honed my craft, offering custom engraving services for various products, from wooden signs to personalized gifts. Word spread quickly, and soon, I found myself inundated with orders.

What started as a side hustle quickly grew into a thriving business. The extra income from my laser engraving venture provided me with the financial stability I had been longing for. No longer was I shackled by the constraints of living paycheck to paycheck. I had finally achieved a sense of freedom and security.

But I didn't stop there. Buoyed by the success of my laser engraving business, I began exploring other entrepreneurial endeavors. I diversified my income streams, seizing opportunities wherever they arose. Before I knew it, I had built a portfolio of successful ventures, each contributing to my financial well-being and personal fulfillment.

Looking back, I'm grateful for the journey that led me to where I am today. Breaking free from the paycheck-to-paycheck cycle wasn't easy, but it was undoubtedly worth it. And it all started with a laser and a dream.

Alright, buckle up because this book is your ticket to financial freedom and entrepreneurial success. Here's what's in store for you:

- **Practical Strategies**: I'll walk you through practical, actionable strategies for managing your money, from budgeting and saving to investing and building wealth. No complicated jargon or boring lectures—just straightforward advice you can start using right away.
- **Mindset Shifts**: We'll dive deep into the mindset shifts and behavioral changes necessary to break free from the paycheck-to-paycheck cycle and adopt the mindset of a successful entrepreneur. **Spoiler alert:** it's all about confidence, determination, and a willingness to take calculated risks.
- **Entrepreneurship 101:** Whether you're a seasoned business pro or a total newbie, I've got you covered. I'll guide you through the basics of starting and running a successful business, from identifying opportunities to marketing your products or services.
- **Actionable Advice:** This isn't just a book you read and forget about. Each chapter is packed with actionable advice and practical exercises to help you apply what you've learned to your own life and business. Think

of it as your personal roadmap to success.

So, what are you waiting for? If you're tired of living paycheck to paycheck and ready to take control of your financial destiny, then this book is for you. By the time you're done reading, you'll have all the tools, knowledge, and inspiration you need to finally break free from the grind and build the life of your dreams. So, grab a copy, dive in, and let's get started on this journey to financial independence together!

1

Chapter 1

Introduction

1.1 Understanding the Cycle of Living Paycheck to Paycheck

Millions of individuals around the world are in the unstable financial predicament of living paycheck to paycheck. Usually at the start of this cycle, people or families spend almost all of their money every pay period, leaving little to nothing saved for savings accounts or investments in the future. The vicious cycle continues as people struggle to pay for necessities of life until their next payday, many turning to credit cards or high-interest loans to get by.

People receive their paychecks at the beginning of the cycle, and they promptly use them to cover necessities like rent or a mortgage, utilities, groceries, and travel expenses. Since they don't have much extra money to spend, unforeseen costs like auto repairs or medical expenditures might easily knock them over budget and increase their debt.

People struggle financially as the pay period goes on because they are trying to stretch their leftover funds until the next paycheck. This may force one to make tough decisions like skipping out on other necessary costs or foregoing wholesome meals or medical attention. The cycle can also be made worse by the pressure to uphold appearances or meet social expectations, which can lead to excessive spending on non-essential goods.

People who don't have enough money saved up or don't have access to credit that can be afforded may turn to high-interest credit cards or payday loans to pay for urgent needs. Although these solutions offer short-term respite, they frequently have astronomical costs and interest rates, which ensnare people in a debt cycle from which it is harder and harder to break free.

Moreover, people who don't have any savings are ill-equipped to deal with unforeseen financial difficulties or emergencies, which feeds the cycle of living paycheck to paycheck. Any progress achieved in breaking free from the cycle is undermined every time an unanticipated expense occurs, leaving people feeling helpless and overwhelmed by their financial situation.

Increasing income, cutting costs, and conserving money all need to be done deliberately in order to break the paycheck to paycheck cycle. This may be looking for jobs that pay more, learning new skills or going to school to increase earning potential, sticking to a strict budget to prioritize necessities, and looking into ways to pay off debt and save money for emergencies.

Causes of Living Paycheck to Paycheck

While the reasons for living paycheck to paycheck can range from one source to another, the situation generally becomes knotted in financial chokepoints. Here are some common causes:

1. Low Wages: One of the principal reasons is poor income. There are people that work in low-paying jobs which do not suffice for basic living expenses, not even talk of any saving for emergencies or the future. It might arise from the limited education or lack of job opportunities, or even the economic crises.

2. High Cost of Living: Rise in housing, healthcare, education, and other necessities prices can easily consume quite a big portion of income. In places where housing costs are high or where affordable housing is limited, individuals often face difficulty managing the rent or mortgage resulting in lack of funds left for other services.

3. Debt: Building up debt, whether credit card or loan debt, or medical bills, will rapidly use up your financial cushion and make it extremely unattractive to try and break the cycle of living paycheck to paycheck. High-interest rates and fees aggravate the problem as borrowers take loans to cover their debts. This causes a borrowing-to-cover your payments cycle.

4. Lack of Savings: If the finances are not secured, people tend to be very susceptible to unforeseen expenses or generation of some other income. The vast majority of people do not have a sufficient amount of savings to pay for an ordinary emergency, so they resort to credit or payday loans for survival.

5. Financial Illiteracy: If you have limited knowledge about budgeting, saving, investing and debt management, you may be making poor financial decisions and on top of that, you may fall into the paycheck to paycheck circle. The absence of the knowledge required to weather financial storms can deny people the opportunity to lay a good financial foundation.

6. Unpredictable Income: Some employees for example in the gig economy or with flexible schedules, have irregular income patterns, hence, they will find it hard to budget and plan for expenditures. Volatility of income could intensify financial instability––and thus increase credit or short-term loans dependence.

7. Health Issues: Medical emergencies and chronic health problems can have major medical expenses and lost income from time off work or being unable to work at all. This can tank people's finances and saddle them deeper into the paycheck-to-paycheck trap.

8. Family Obligations: Family members including children, parents old in age or other relatives may add some financial burden on an individual. Childcare outlays, education costs, and the need to care for others have an additional effect on the available income and take away from a financial progression.

It is not enough to just address the underlying causes of the payday-to-payday cycle without a holistic approach that includes policies to deal with income inequality, housing and healthcare affordability initiatives, consumer protection policies, and financial education and literacy programs. Besides, people can improve their financial standing through increasing income, causing expenses to go down, managing debt, and saving up money slowly but steadily.

Impact on Financial Stability

Living from one paycheck to another can have a profound effect on individuals and their families, influencing several facets of their existence.

1. Financial Stress: The persistent concern about meeting financial obligations and covering essential expenses can lead to financial stress. This stress can exert a substantial impact on mental well-being, leading to symptoms such as anxiety, melancholy, and other disorders.

2. Restricted Financing Alternatives: The expenses associated with payment are exceedingly minimal, leading to negligible savings. This hampers individuals' ability to make financial decisions such as pursuing further education, engaging in real estate investments, or saving for retirement.

3. Accumulated Debt: In situations where customers lack alternative choices, they may resort to utilizing credit cards, payday loans, or other forms of high-interest debt in order to meet unexpected needs. This creates a pernicious loop of accumulating debt, rendering it arduous to sustain a lifestyle reliant on each successive income.

4. Lack of financial savings: The absence of the capacity to save and invest money hinders individuals from accumulating wealth or enhancing their financial situation. They could be caught in a relentless cycle of financial instability that prevents them from achieving long-term financial goals, such as owning a home or saving for retirement.

5. Limited access to resources: Pay-to-pay may restrict access to key resources and services. People may struggle to pay for health care, education, housing, and transportation, worsening the cycle of poverty and lack of income.

6. Increased Vulnerability to unexpected Events: Without savings, people are unprepared to meet unforeseen costs such as medical bills, automotive repairs, or job loss. This disease leads to other obstacles, especially financial ones.

7. Effect on Relationships: Financial stress may have an effect on your relationships with family, friends, and loved ones. Disputes about money, changes in spending patterns, and the inability to support common events may all produce pressure and stress in relationships.

8. Job mobility is restricted: Financial uncertainties can hamper career progress and mobility. People may be unable to invest in education or training to upgrade their skills and credentials, restricting their earning potential and work possibilities. In general, the livable wage restricts a person's financial independence, possibilities, and livelihood.

9. The biggest danger of homelessness: People who live paycheck to paycheck are more likely to face eviction and end up homeless if they don't have a healthy budget and savings for housing necessities. This is particularly valid during difficult financial or economic circumstances.

10. Effects on Health: People with low incomes put off or disregard medical

care and preventive measures due to cost concerns. This may result in untreated medical conditions, poorer health outcomes, and higher long-term medical expenses.

11. Financial Goals Are Hard to Achieve: Long-term financial objectives like saving for a home, launching a business, or applying to college are unlikely to be met if one is continuously unable to pay for essentials. Depression and feelings of uncertainty may result from this.

12. Effects on mental health: Low self-esteem, insecurity, and hopelessness might result from being paid to pay. Long-term worry and stress brought on by unstable finances might worsen mental health.

13. Restricted Educational Options: People with limited resources may not be able to pursue schooling that will advance their careers or lead to well-paying jobs. This keeps people in a loop of low income and unstable finances.

14. Suffocated self-development: Efforts to better oneself may be hampered by a lack of funds. Books, seminars, and other experiences that are good for personal development and enrichment might not be affordable for certain people.

15. Impact on Children: Stress and uncertainty are common among children raised in families where both parents work. Education, health, and general well-being are negatively impacted by inadequate financial support, which in turn affects opportunities and results.

16. Excess mental bandwidth: People with low mental resources are forced to concentrate on other significant aspects of their lives, such as employment, relationships, and personal development, because ongoing financial concerns reduce mental bandwidth.

17. Investment Analysis: People lose their financial freedom and become dependent on others, including family members, on government assistance programs when they don't have savings or investment options.

18. Impact on Retirement Planning: People shouldn't be prepared for retirement since living paycheck to paycheck implies ignoring retirement savings and depending on Social Security or other sources of financial help in the future.

19. Social isolation: Being unable to participate in social activities or events that require spending money is a result of financial instability, which causes retreat and social isolation. Loneliness and isolation rise as a result.These consequences underscore the need to solve underlying problems and guarantee the financial stability of both individuals and society. They also demonstrate the vast range of difficulties and implications of the living wage on benefits.

Breaking free from the Cycle

Getting out of the paycheck-to-paycheck lifestyle involves a mix of planning, saving, and boosting your income if needed. Here are some strategies:

1. Create a Budget: Track your expenditure and income to get knowledge of where your money is directed. Split your income into items you need such as rent, utilities, groceries, and payment for transportation and save some and use the remaining to pay debts.

2. Emergency Fund: Create an emergency fund that would cover the car repairing or any medical bills you happen to incur. At least three to six months salary or living expenses.

3. Cut Expenses: Seek out the areas where you can trim your expenses. Discretionary spending cuts include dining out, entertainment, and subscription

services.

4. Increase Income: Take time to check out ways you can improve your income, such as requesting a salary raise, getting another job that pays more than your previous one or getting another job on the side to earn extra or looking for freelance work.

5. Debt Management: Create a plan of how to pay off high interest debts. Try the debt snowball (pay off the lower balances first) or debt avalanche (pay off the highest interest first).

6. Live Below Your Means: Do not fall into the lifestyle inflation trap. Say 'No way!' to your increased income temptation of spending spiraling upwards. Instead, continue to live below your means and allocate more savings and investments.

7. Automate Savings: Make sure to build automatic transfers to your savings account to build an amount through each and every month.

8. Track Progress: Keep an eye on your financial progress on a regular basis so that you could remain motivated and change anything if necessary. Celebrate milestones that come your way as you work your way to financial stability.

9. Prioritize High-Interest Debt: Paying off debt with a high interest rate should be considered a very big priority, as the interest can slowly but surely lead to severe financial restrictions. That could include the credit cards as well as payday loans.

10. Negotiate Bills: Consult the service vendors like cable, internet and also the insurance companies to bring down the costs. One of the ways is to get discounts and many promotions from the providers for the loyal customers.

11. Use Cash Envelopes: Designated money for the variable expenses, including groceries, dining out, and also entertainment. Cash envelopes can act as a very fiscally responsible guide and also help prevent you from going over the budget.

12. Seek Financial Education: Financial literacy is an investment which can contribute to your better comprehension of your own personal financial matters such as investing, savings and also budgeting. Resources are composed of many books, podcasts, online courses and also workshops.

13. Consider Housing Options: Assess your accommodation arrangements to check that there is anything you can do to save some money. This may mean moving into a much smaller place or an apartment, sharing a house with a roommate or negotiating with your landlord for a rent reduction.

14. Explore Government Assistance Programs: Check into the government's many assistance programs that are provided for the needy. These include the households' assistance, food stamps, or even childcare vouchers. These programs can give you an opportunity to receive some support and a helping hand as you strive to become financially very stable.

15. Set Financial Goals: Set up both short-term and also long-term financial objectives that inform your decisions and put you in the right order of importance regarding your spending. Whether it is a down payment on a house, student loan payments or saving for retirement, clear goals help you to live a disciplined and focused life.

16. Stay Flexible: Be flexible with your financial plan as many events take place. An example of financial matters that will change your budget or savings plan may include job loss, illness or unanticipated expenses. There are two very essential qualities to overcome as the financial challenges that a company will face.

1.2 Why Money Mastery is Essential for Financial Freedom

Money mastery is a key component of financial freedom since by mastering money, one can effectively manage their finances, make wise decisions, and grow their wealth in the long run. Here's why:

1. Financial Awareness: Financial independence is an event about knowing your income level, living expenses, assets and debts. With that in mind, you can take action to pinpoint the aspects that require your attention, follow your progress, and undertake necessary changes.

2. Budgeting and Planning: Skills in financial management allow you to put together and discharge a budget reflecting your financial objectives. Through precise planning of your spending and saving, you can establish the order of importance and avoid the unnecessary expenditure on the things that are not so essential.

3. Debt Management: Knowing how to deal with and extinguish debt is very important in gaining financial independence. Financial literacy pertains to learning techniques to handle debt effectively, for example, the debt snowball and paying extra installments whenever an opportunity exists.

4. Saving and Investing: Effective control of finance is financial planning and budgeting in order to accumulate wealth. If you save for emergencies, retirement and other long-term goals, you have a chance for financial security and freedom.

5. Risk Management: Financial literacy is a combination of understanding the risks and those factors that counter them in order not to jeopardize your financial well-being. This can include ensuring you have enough insurance coverage, varying your investments, and having a savings account that you reserve for emergencies only.

6. Maximizing Income: Money sense is attained by any or all of the following ways - career advancement for salary increment, side hustles, putting your money in the right investments or starting a business. To fasten your way out of bondage and into financial freedom, you need to optimize your earning potential.

7. Lifestyle Design: dominance over financial resources provides you with the capacity to model your lifestyle to suit your principles and ambitions. You have become free from being controlled by money or finances, which means you have the right to make your own decision on how to live or spend your time.

8. Generational Wealth: Building wealth through money mastery not only benefits you but also future generations. By passing on financial knowledge, resources, and values to your children and grandchildren, you can create a legacy of prosperity and opportunity.

9. Reduced Stress: Having mastery over your money reduces financial stress and anxiety, allowing you to focus on other aspects of your life with greater peace of mind.

10. Opportunity Seizing: Financial mastery enables you to seize opportunities when they arise, whether it's investing in a promising venture, purchasing a property at a favorable price, or pursuing further education or training.

11. Independence: Achieving financial mastery grants you greater independence and autonomy in decision-making, freeing you from reliance on others for financial support or approval.

12. Retirement Planning: Mastery over money allows you to plan for a comfortable retirement by saving and investing strategically, ensuring you have the resources to enjoy your golden years without financial worries.

13. Education and Growth: Financial mastery often involves continuous learning and personal growth as you seek to improve your financial literacy, skills, and mindset, leading to greater self-confidence and fulfillment.

14. Philanthropy and Giving Back: With financial freedom comes the ability to give back to causes and communities that are important to you, making a positive impact and leaving a legacy of generosity and compassion.

15. Resilience: Mastery over money builds resilience, equipping you with the knowledge and resources to weather financial setbacks and challenges that may arise throughout your life.

16. Empowerment: Being in control of your finances empowers you to pursue your passions, dreams, and aspirations without being hindered by financial constraints or limitations.

17. Wealth Preservation: Financial mastery involves strategies for preserving and growing your wealth over the long term, ensuring that you can sustain your lifestyle and provide for future generations.

18. Peace of Mind for Loved Ones: Achieving financial mastery not only benefits you but also your loved ones, providing them with greater financial security and peace of mind knowing that you have planned for their future well-being.

By mastering your money, you can unlock a world of opportunities, security, and fulfillment, ultimately leading to a life of greater freedom and abundance.

1.3 Tracking Income and Expenses

Properly recording your income and expenses is essential for gaining understanding of your long term financial behavior and for making sound financial decisions. Here's how to do it effectively:

1. Choose a Tracking Method: Pick out a tracking approach that fits best your needs. You may use a spreadsheet, a budgeting software, a mobile app, or handwritten notes. Select the approach you can take and that you will use consistently.

2. Record Your Income: Begin by listing each source of income; you can include salaries, wages, bonuses, freelancing and any other type of income that is applicable. Ensure that you consider taxes and deductions in the case you have to adjust your income to the net.

3. List Your Expenses: Classify your expenses in a fixed and a variable category. The amount that does not change regardless of the business model, process or technique used is fixed costs and this includes rent or mortgage, utilities, insurance and loan payments. The expenses of a variable nature are the groceries, dining out, entertainment, transportation and personal spending.

4. Track Every Transaction: Keep the trace of the transaction no matter how large or small it is. Retaining receipts, online banking solutions, or setting up alerts will help you track your expenses in real time. This will help you visualize your money outflow.

5. Categorize Your Expenses: Designate one category to every transaction for you to identify your spending habits. The following are common categories: housing, transportation, food, utilities, payments for debts, entertainment, and savings.

6. Set Budgets: Reflecting on your income and expenses, create reasonable budgets for every category. Your objective should be a sizable portion of your income be set aside towards necessities such as housing and utilities, and prioritize savings and debt repayment.

7. Review Regularly: Consider your income and expenses regularly to

check whether you are on a budget. Find any spots where you could be overspending or where you can cut back on some of your costs, and make changes as necessary.

8. Track Trends Over Time: Look for trends in your spending habits over time. Are there months where you consistently overspend? Are there areas where you consistently underspend? Use this information to make improvements to your budget and financial habits.

9. Use Tools and Technology: Try out budgeting apps and online tools that make the tracking easier and have a feature that provides information about your spending habits. Some apps automatically categorize the transactions and provide graphs and charts that depict the financial data.

10. Be Consistent: Consistency is the main prerequisite for successful monitoring. Whatever frequency you would like (either daily, weekly or monthly) ,make recording of your income and expenses a habit. The more you maintain your consistency, the better knowledge you'll gain about the state of your financial status.

11. Use Separate Accounts: Think about the separate bank accounts with different purposes, such as pay bills as well as fixed expenses, use the other account in savings goals, and lastly spending discretionary. This is how you will be able to monitor your finances properly and keep going.

12. Track Cash Spending: Also, if you in most cases use cash for transactions, keep the good habit of tracking these expenses too. To record a cash sale is benefitting to keep a little notebook or to use a mobile app, and to do it at once when the sale happens.

13. Review Statements Regularly: Take some time off to review all your bank and credit card statements with regular intervals to make sure that all the transactions are properly recorded. Keep an eye on any inconsistencies or

any charges you don't authorize and address them right away.

14. Utilize Tags or Labels: Some types of budgeting software permit you to add labels or tags to transactions, which could include for example if they were for personal or business purposes, specific projects or categories. Use these characteristics to create a richer context in your spending history.

15. Automate Recurring Payments: Create standing orders for regular expenses such as rent, utility bills and loan payments to aid in timely payment each month. This is one way that you can avoid late fees while also making the budgeting process easier.

16. Track Non-Monthly Expenses: Be sure to include the additional annual expenses, such as annual subscriptions, quarterly insurance premiums, or bi-annual property taxes. Place funds to cover these expenses in your budget and every month allot money to cover them when they fall due.

17. Track Your Net Worth: Tracking your income as well as expenditure, from time to time, calculate your net worth by subtracting your liabilities (debts) from your assets. The monitoring of your net worth over time is very valuable in providing insights into your financial condition and how well you are doing on your financial goals.

18. Review Your Goals Regularly: Always refresh your financial objectives and modify your budget and spending pattern as necessitated by. Do you believe you are on budget to meet up with your savings goals? Are you required to recalibrate your budget to give certain expenses or savings goals preference?

19. Involve Your Family: If you share the financial issues of your partner or family members, let them be a part of budgeting and tracking processes. A regular meeting to share and discuss your financial goals and progress is highly recommended. This way, everyone is on the same page.

20. Seek Accountability: Seek for an accountability partner or join a financial community where you can share your report, issues and successes. Having a person with you, who will be there for you and motivate and inspire you, can help you create yourself a road map to achieve your financial ambitions.

By diligently tracking your income and expenses, you will be able to gather invaluable information about your financial patterns and will be in a better position to make data-driven decisions on your money in order to ultimately reach your financial goals.

1.4 Understanding the Importance of Financial Planning

Financial planning is crucial for several reasons:

1. Goal Achievement: The process enables many people and companies to set measurable financial objectives and to plan ways of achieving them. It may be needed for saving for retirement, for buying a house, or financing education.

2. Risk Management: Financial planning serves to determine the future risks and find ways to avoid them, avoiding insurance or diversifying the investments into various markets being some of them.

3. Budgeting and Cash Flow Management: Through the development of a budget and the tracking of the money coming in and out, financial planning pays a lot of attention to how the income is divided between spending, savings, and investments so as to prevent the accumulating of debt and to build wealth.

4. Tax Efficiency: Financial planning done efficiently will lead to the reduction of the tax liability through the methods such as tax-deferred investments, tax deductions and credits, ultimately optimizing the wealth creation.

5. Retirement Planning: It allows people to determine how much to save for retirement and creates a plan to meet that goal, thereby ensuring that one has the retirement life which they dreamed of.

6. Investment Strategy: Economic planning helps in forming an investment portfolio that is consistent with one's patience in regard to the risk, the period for which one will require funds, and the financial objectives one intends to meet, balancing returns and managing risk.

7. Estate Planning: It includes putting things in the order, laying down plans for the disposal of assets after death, minimizing the taxes and also ensuring the transfer of assets is done within the capacity of the individual.

8. Financial Security: In general, financial planning is the key to the budgeting that ensures people and companies have control over their finances. Financial planning helps to reduce the personal and also business financial uncertainty and build a good financial base for the future.

Certainly, here's one more importance of financial planning:

9. Peace of Mind for Loved Ones: Through proper estate planning and insurance coverage, financial planning provides peace of mind by ensuring that loved ones are taken care of in the event of disability, illness, or death, alleviating financial burdens and uncertainties during difficult times.

10. Debt Management: Debt can be effectively decreased and controlled through the process of renegotiating terms, consolidating loans, and giving priority to obligations with high interest rates. Not only does this enhance financial well-being, but it also decreases loan interest.

11. Enhanced Decision-Making: Individuals who actively participate in financial planning possess the necessary knowledge and skills to make educated decisions that optimize potential gains while limiting potential risks. This is particularly beneficial when facing significant financial choices,

such as purchasing a property, launching a business, or pursuing advanced education.

12. Lifestyle Maintenance: A key objective of financial planning is to ensure that income and expenses are balanced, enabling individuals to sustain their existing lifestyle without excessive spending or jeopardizing their long-term financial objectives.

13. Millionaire's Management specializes in the preservation and growth of intergenerational wealth, ensuring a reliable income stream for both present and future generations.

14. Adaptability and Flexibility: To ensure that a person can keep financial stability and develop toward their objective, financial planning should be adaptive enough to account for life's changes, such as job loss, marriage, divorce, or unforeseen financial occurrences.

15. Psychological Well-Being: A strong financial plan may remove a lot of the tension and anxiety that comes with money management, leading to a sense of mastery, confidence, and general enjoyment of life.

17. Social Responsibility: A financial plan allows people to set aside money for charitable donations, volunteer activities, or ethical investing, all of which can have an impact on the environment and society.

Overall, financial planning is vital in supporting individuals and organizations in navigating the nuances of their financial situations, reaching their goals, and guaranteeing a safe and prosperous future.

1.5 Setting Financial Goals

The establishment of financial goals is a foundation of financial planning. Here's why it's important and how to do it effectively:

1. Clarity and Focus: Establishing specific financial targets leads the way, creates a sense of purpose, and also helps the one or an organization to concentrate on the most important matters at hand.

2. Motivation: A goal with a clear financial meaning e.g. saving for a vacation, can really stimulate the motivation, which supports disciplined saving, investment, and spending activities intended to realize that goal.

3. Measurement of Progress: Financial goals provide a very good basis for measuring the progress and success, helping the individuals determine their financial state and then make changes if necessary to remain on the track.

4. Decision Making: Financial goals defined in a clear manner allows for the informed decision making in regards to the budgeting, investing, and other financial matters so that the decisions are aligned with the ultimate objectives.

5. Time Horizon: Financial goals are commonly classified by the horizon in the time, namely short-term (less than one year), medium-term (one to five years) and also long-term (more than five years), thereby to facilitate the way of planning and investment.

6. Specificity: The financial goals must be very specific, measurable, achievable, relevant and also time-bound (SMART), because they are the ones that give a clear plan of action and also evaluation.

7. Identify Objectives: Figure out what you want to finance in the future, such as save for retirement, purchase a home, pay off debt or fund your

education.

8. Quantify Goals: To make them up to measure and also achievable, set specific dollar amounts and timelines for each financial goal.

9. Prioritize Goals: Set priorities among the financial goals based on the importance and also urgency of them, factoring in interest rates, time horizon, personal values and so on.

10. Break Down Goals: If long-term goals seem over powering, restate them using smaller and also more achievable milestones so as to track the progress and stay motivated.

11. Review and Adjust: Schedule periodic reviews of the financial objectives, and make revisions / updates to them where appropriate, as the circumstances / priorities change / market conditions evolve.

12. Resource Allocation: Financial goals (in other words – managing resources efficiently) provide a way to channelize the financial flows so that money is channeled to the most meaningful objectives; instead of being spent randomly.

13. Risk Management:For financial goal setting, one should consider risks and create strategies to reduce them, such as asset diversification or insurance provision.

14. Financial Discipline: A disciplined approach to money management results from having clear financial goals. Being consistent in budgeting, saving, and investing efforts to realize those goals are some of the habits it can promote.

15. Financial Independence:Setting and meeting financial goals can result in more financial independence, lessening the need for dependency on external

support and the freedom to make decisions about one's money without relying on outsiders significantly.

16. Adaptability:The financial goals can be fine-tuned as time goes on to depict the changes in circumstances, priorities, and preferences, ensuring flexibility and yet maintaining a sense of direction and purpose.

17. Opportunity Identification:** The financial goals are clearly defined to individuals and businesses in order to identify the chances that fit into their objectives such as taking benefits of investment opportunities or achieving career advancements **

18. Financial Awareness:The process of establishing financial goals builds the higher awareness of one's financial condition including income, expenses, assets, and liabilities which consequently equals to the improved financial decisions.

19. Long-Term Vision: Financial goals outline a long-term vision for financial success, and in turn, short-term actions and decisions are in line with them to achieve that success in a sustainable way.

20. Psychological Benefits: Financial goals achieved can promote confidence, self-esteem and wholesome well-being providing a sense of accomplishment and contentment towards the realization of key objectives.

21. Legacy Planning:Financial goals extend even beyond one's lifetime because they may consist of objectives that go beyond the individual like charity, estate planning or the family wealth succession plan.

2

Chapter 2

Creating a Budget that Works for You

2.1 What is a Budget?

B udget is a roadmap for the winning strategy in finance, where all the income and spending is worked out systematically. Budget, basically, is a list of expected incomes and the required outflows over an assigned duration, mostly a month or a year. It gives a structure that helps the individuals, families, businesses or also governments to decide where to spend the money on resource allocation efficiently, and accomplish the financial objectives.

Creating a budget means estimating all the sources of income that come from a salary, investment or any other earnings, and categorizing the expenses as fixed and variable (e.g., rent, loan payments for the first one and groceries, entertainment for the second one). Through the comparison of projected income with the scheduled expenses, one can identify the areas with the potential for savings or changes that are very necessary. Budgeting is financial discipline development by planning one spend thoughtfully while curbing any impulsive decisions.

2.2 Why is Budgeting Important?

Budgeting is crucial for various reasons:

1. Financial Control: Planning option to let you see how all your money you make and spend comes to be, giving you an overall picture of your finances, thus, allowing you to manage your own personal finances. It gives you an image of all your revenue outflow and how to change and achieve your finance target.

2. Goal Setting: Budgeting is the tool that allows you to define the financial goals and choose which one to start with – the savings for a vacation, a new house or your debts payoff. Performing this resource allocation will bring you more forward to the accomplishment of them.

3. Emergency Preparedness: Budgeting plan is there to make you save for those emergencies expenses or needs. This can save you from stress and can also help you to escape the vigil and tough times when the going is very difficult.

4. Debt Management: Budgetary allocation will, therefore, make it possible to locate those areas where you can minimize the spending and then channel the extra income towards clearing the debt. By an adequate regulation of debts the interest payable can be reduced significantly and the time of becoming debt-free can be greatly decreased.

5. Improved Decision Making: The clarity we gain with budgeting of the financial condition enables us to make financial decisions that are informed, since it will also be easier for us to select how to spend, save and even invest. So, in the long run it may lead to better financial results and therefore also stability.

6. Behavioral Awareness: Budgeting makes you think about your spending

patterns and also discover where you tend to spend too much money or make spontaneous buys. With this awareness, you might adjust your financial behavior accordingly, for example by cutting down on some of the unnecessary expenses, and also by becoming more intentional about the way you spend.

7. Financial Planning: One of the most important parts of financial planning is budgeting. Through creating a budget, you can evaluate your own current financial situation, detect the weak spots and get a plan for your future financial prosperity.

8. Risk Management: Budgeting helps you to assess the risks and take necessary steps to avert the financial risks. Through developing a really good picture of what you earn and spend, you can create savings funds to help cope with the unplanned, such as losing a job, a medical emergency, or having to repair something expensive.

9. Increased Savings: Budgeting enables you to transfer some of your income to the savings and investments at scheduled intervals. In the long run, you may use this fixated approach to become very rich, acquire assets and attain financial autonomy.

10. Stress Reduction: Financial stress could be very serious for your general well-being. With the creation and adherence to your budget, money matters anxiety can be considerably reduced, and as a result, mental and emotional wellbeing is considerably improved.

11. Financial Accountability: Budgeting is a way of holding you personally accountable for your own financial actions and also keeping you on track towards achieving your goals. You will be able to keep yourself motivated when you regularly review your budget and also closely monitor your direction of the progress. And you can always make the appropriate adjustments to your financial path to stay in line with your financial goals.

12. Improved Relationships: According to budgeting, relationships will benefit from this. It will greatly benefit the relationship that involves shared finance. Through creating a budget jointly, couples and families should discuss openly their financial goals, priorities, and concerns that will result in their better relationships and conflicts on finance.

13. Financial Education: Participation in budgeting provides a chance of mastering personal financial issues (budgeting procedures, saving tactics, debt solutions, investment concepts). This knowledge equips you with the tool of making wise financial choices at any stage of your life.

14. Long-Term Wealth Building: Budgeting provides a habit of systematic savings and investment, which is essential for long-term wealth growth. By allocating resources prudently along the retirement accounts, equities, real estate, and other assets you can grow wealth and secure your income.

15. Adaptability: A good budget design will help you to adapt to financial difficulties that crop up. Either you get an increase in your income or encounter sudden expenses or new goals, the budget is a tool that helps you change your spending and saving as needed.

16. Financial Freedom: Budget eventually is a method to get financial freedom. Through proper money management, lowering debt and setting up savings, you can control your life choices, which will allow you to pursue your vocational ambitions, personal interests and passions without depending on financial restrictions.

In a nutshell, budgeting is a very powerful instrument that allows you to make many better decisions, while moving closer to a financially resilient and also plentiful future.

2.3 Developing a Budget Plan

Developing a budget plan involves several steps:

1. Set Financial Goals: Determine what your short term, medium term and long term financial goals are. Such could be debt relief, vacation saving, buying a house, or creating an emergency fund.

2. Assess Your Income: Calculate the total monthly income from all sources (your salary, bonus, freelance work and rent and any other revenues.).

3. Track Your Expenses: Go back over your expenses from the past to understand where your money has been going. Separate your expenses into two categories, that is, fixed (e.g., rent, utility bills) and variable (e.g., groceries, entertainment).

4. Identify Areas for Adjustment: Break down your expenses to spot eating out every day or buying expensive clothes with alarming frequency. Find the excess expenses that can be cut without the major changes in the quality of life.

5. Allocate Funds: Spend your money on various kinds of expense groups based on your needs and financial goals. Ensure that cash is available for the proper expenses including essential, debt repayment, savings, and discretionary spending.

6. Create a Budget Template: Using a spreadsheet,app or paper and pen make a budget template. At the top of the list enumerate your income and then subtract your expenses so as to determine your net income or surplus.

7. Track Your Progress: Regularly monitor your spending going with your budgeted amounts. Alter your budget depending upon variants in your income, expenses, or financial goals.

8. Build an Emergency Fund: Invest money into a stash-fund intended to cover any unforeseen expenses or financial situations that come up. Your goal should be saving enough to live for three to six months in a liquid savings account.

9. Plan for Debt Repayment: Pay up high-interest debt first if you have debt. Use your additional income you are receiving for paying your debt. Consider the debt snowball and debt avalanche strategies to expedite your transition from debt.

10. Review and Adjust: Periodically review your budget to assess your progress towards your financial goals and make adjustments as needed. Celebrate your achievements and stay committed to your long-term financial success.

11. Automate Savings and Bill Payments: Set up an automatic transfer from your checking account to your savings or investment accounts every month. This way you ensure that money is allocated for savings. In like manner, pay bills automatically to dodge potential late fees and missed payments.

12. Use Cash Envelopes:You may employ the cash envelope system for some categories of expenditure, i.e., groceries or entertainment. Bungi a certain amount of money on every envelope every month and then only spend what money that you have in each envelope.

13. Review Subscriptions and Memberships: Perform periodical reviews of your subscriptions, memberships, and recurring expenses to validate whether or not they are the right option for you. Stop any service agreements that you are no longer using to channel the funds to other goals.

14. Plan for Irregular Expenses: Create a fund for the unusual expenses and save for that. For example, your annual insurance premiums, car maintenance and holiday gifts. Establish a nest egg of some of your revenues each month

so that you are financially ready when the time comes.

15. Consider Multiple Income Streams: Find chances to grow your earned income by doing some freelance work, side job, or getting passive income streams. Dedicate any excess income toward savings, debt, or investment for acceleration of financial growth.

16. Stay Flexible: Be flexible and ready for adaptation to your budgeting plan. Circumstances of life and financial priorities may change with time, so it is advisable to be ready to revisit your budget every now and then to incorporate your current situation and goals.

17. Track Your Net Worth: Track your personal wealth periodically through your assets and liabilities stockpiling. Doing this can give you a full picture of your financial health and moving forward, a few steps at a time to achieve wealth.

18. Seek Accountability: Share with a close friend or a family member the budgeting goals and your progress. A trusted advisor who will listen, support and hold you accountable will help you. An accountability partner can always give you the necessary motivation when you need it and hold you accountable to your financial goals.

2.4 Monitoring and Managing Your Budget

Monitoring and managing your budget will be an extremely important ingredient when you are trying to accomplish your financial goals. Here's how to effectively monitor and manage your budget:

1. Regularly Track Expenses: Watch over your spending by recording what you spend from the time to time. Budgeting apps, spreadsheets or even pen and papers will be able to help you in recording all your spending and also receive payments. This will give an opportunity to you and also know

whether you are overspending any place where you can cut back can be identified.

2. Review Your Budget Frequently: Take time at least once every week or once a month to check on your budgeting. Make a comparison of your real expenditure to your planned expenses and check using your progress towards the financial goals you set. Make amendments as needed to keep the company in line with your objective.

3. Stay Disciplined: Stay committed to the budget by adopting self-discipline and not giving into the temptations of impulse purchases. Prior to buying a non-essential item, consider whether it will contribute to achieving your financial goals and also be in accordance with your budget.

4. Address Budget Variances: Compare the budgeted and the actual expenses if there is a difference in such amounts huge enough to be important, and look for the reasons for their differences. Establish if the reasons behind the variation were the error(s), cost overruns, or income change. Adjust your budget or spending habits, as the case may require, for a continuation of such variances in the days to come.

5. Use Budgeting Tools: Make use of the budgeting tools and resources to greatly simplify the budgeting. Most online platforms and apps feature cost trackers, category budget capacity, and also financial reporting to enable you to easily monitor and manage your budget.

6. Monitor Debt Repayment: If you're working on having no debt, watch your progress for the debt eradication. Keep track of your current balances, APRs, and due dates. Think about using the debt pay-off calculators or apps in order to see what your debt-free path is like and stay very motivated.

7. Save for the Future: Give priority to the saving of the funds for your final financial goals, those that may include building a treasury of emergency fund,

retirement setting aside savings, or making large purchases. Create specific saving targets and consistently contribute to your saving accounts so as to always monitor yourself and make sure you're progressing towards achieving your goals.

8. Stay Flexible: It is possible that over the span of time the circumstances of life and the priorities will change, so take this into account and make revisions with your budget. Keeping flexible and also open-minded, be ready to make amendments to your budget as necessary depending on the emergency expenses of changes in income.

9. Celebrate Successes: Praise and value your small victories as you move towards the target. Whether you have achieved a savings milestone, paid off a credit card debt, or budgeted repeatedly, take time to appreciate your success and keep on fighting to continue your financial journey.

10. Use Cash Flow Forecasting: Forecast future income and expenses to predict changes in cash flow. This will help you plan for upcoming expenses, reduce cash flow, and ensure you have enough money to meet your financial obligations.

11. Consider financial reports: Prepare periodic financial reports, such as income statements, balance sheets, and cash flow statements, to understand your financial health. Analyze key financial metrics and trends to identify opportunities for improvement and make decisions.

12. Practice Frugality: Develop lifestyle strategies to reduce costs and increase savings. Find ways to reduce the cost of common expenses such as food, cars and utilities. To save money, consider DIY solutions, buy used items, or choose a better deal.

13. Define expenses Agree: Provide expenses for overdue expenses to avoid expenses. Use methods such as portfolios, sinking funds, or spending to

enforce these limits and ensure you stick to your budgeted amount.

14. Monitor Net Worth: Monitor your net worth regularly by checking the difference between your assets (eg savings, investments, property) and liabilities (eg debts, loans). Tracking your net income over time will help you measure your financial progress and make decisions about wealth building strategies.

15. Use Alerts and Reminders: Set up alerts and reminders to notify you of payment due dates, low account balances, and unusual spending situations. This can help you stay organized, avoid late payments, and resolve difficulties ahead of time.

16. Find Pills and Deals: Complete assessments of your bills and expenses to identify savings. Consider exchanging with your service provider or more to a lower location to reduce your expense.

17. Monitor Your Credit Score: Continue to monitor your credit score and credit report to ensure your financial behavior is positively impacting your creditworthiness. Check your credit report for errors or misses, and have a way to keep it.

18. Use Procrastination Analysis: Determine how to procrastinate the need by prioritizing long-term financial goals over short-term needs. Deferring interest can help you make better purchasing decisions and keep you focused on achieving your financial goals.

19. Seek Professional Advice: If you are having trouble managing your budget or meeting your financial goals, consider seeking the advice of a professional or financial advisor. They can provide specific guidance, provide improvement strategies, and help you create a plan for financial success.By implementing these additional strategies into your tracking and management process, you can increase your financial literacy, optimize your spending

habits, and work towards achieving financial and life security..

Through making sound budgetary monitoring and also management practices a habit, you will get the financial stability back, will be able to choose the right direction and act towards accomplishing your current and also future financial goals.

2.5 Choosing a Budget Method

2.5.1 The Zero-based Budgeting

The zero-based budgeting (ZBB) approach to budgeting means having no revenue and no expenses. This implies that every dollar you make serves a purpose, be it debt reduction, investing, saving, or consuming.

Principles and Concept of Zero-based Budgeting

1. Every Dollar Has a Purpose: In ZBB, each and every dollar of revenue is earmarked for a certain debt repayment, investment, savings target, or expense. This guarantees the effective and efficient utilization of all revenue.

2. Start from Zero: ZBB begins each budgeting period from scratch, in contrast to standard budgeting techniques that use prior budgets as a foundation. This implies that regardless of whether they were covered by prior budgets, spending needs to be justified and approved for each quarter.

3. Decision Packages: Costs are grouped into decision packages, which are financing requests for certain projects or initiatives. A description of the activity, its goals, the resources needed, and the anticipated results or advantages are all included in each decision package.

4. Focus on Value: ZBB promotes concentrating on the significance and worth of every expenditure. ZBB encourages managers to justify and

prioritize expenses based on how they contribute to corporate goals and objectives, rather than just carrying over existing spending.

5. Incremental vs. Zero-based Thinking: Conventional budgetary techniques frequently depend on making small adjustments to earlier budgets. ZBB, on the other hand, promotes zero-based thinking, requiring managers to provide a justification for each spending, even if it was previously budgeted for.

6. Continuous Improvement: ZBB encourages managers to critically assess costs, spot inefficiencies, and look for chances to save money or reallocate resources in order to foster a culture of continuous improvement.

7. Alignment with Strategic Goals: ZBB makes sure that budgetary choices are in line with strategic aims and goals. Allocating resources in a way that optimizes value and supports strategic efforts is made easier with ZBB's requirement that managers explain expenses based on how they contribute to organizational priorities.

Zero-based budgeting is a potent tool for businesses looking to maximize resource allocation and enhance financial management since its guiding principles and concepts prioritize accountability, efficiency, and strategic alignment.

Implementing of Zero-based Budgeting

There are multiple processes involved in implementing zero-based budgeting:

1. Identify Goals and Objectives: This can be putting money aside for unexpected expenses, clearing debt, or making a particular purchase.

2. Include Bills: Make a detailed record of every expense you incur, including both variable and fixed costs (such as groceries and entertainment) as well as

constant costs (like utilities and rent or a mortgage).

3. Assign Currency Values: Determine the total amount of each expense category by looking at your past spending trends and financial objectives. Make sure that each and every dollar of income is attributed to a certain area of spending.

4. Examine and Sort by Priority: Prioritize your expenses according to your financial objectives after evaluating each category to ascertain its necessity. If there are costs that are not necessary or in line with your priorities, think about eliminating or lowering them.

5. Observe and Track: To make sure you're remaining under your spending limit, often monitor your expenditures. Adapt allocations as necessary in light of evolving costs or income.

6. Examine and Modify: Review your budget on a regular basis to see how you're doing financially and make any required adjustments. Be adaptable and ready to change your budget when circumstances do.

7. Talk and Work Together: Include everyone in the budgeting process if you're budgeting as a household, and keep open lines of communication on financial decisions and priorities.

8. Remain Disciplined: Adhere to your spending plan and withstand the urge to go overboard. Keep in mind that implementing a zero-based budget needs dedication and self-control in order to spend every dollar sensibly.

Benefits of Zero-based Budgeting

The following are the benefits of a zero-sum budget:

1. Additional benefits: A zero-sum budget encourages greater accountability for spending decisions throughout the company because all costs must be

calculated and distributed.

2. Cost Savings: A no-nonsense budget can save costs by assessing costs and planning based on strategic needs and goals to eliminate unnecessary expenses.

3. Goal Aligned: Because each expense must be aligned and allocated to a specific project or activity, zero-based budgeting ensures that resources are allocated based on corporate goals and priorities.

4. Optimized Resource Allocation: Resources can be used effectively and efficiently when allocated based on current goals and needs rather than current spending patterns.

5. Encourages Innovation: The non-profit budget encourages creativity and the ability to find solutions to achieve goals with a small amount of money because it starts from part of each period.

6. Improve decision analysis: A zero-sum budget is a solid foundation for resource allocation and decision-making by clarifying the costs and benefits of each expenditure.

7. Adaptation and Response: Nonprofit budgets are reviewed and updated based on current needs and goals, allowing businesses to respond quickly to changing situations and events.

8. Improve communication and clarity: The budget process and interagency collaboration and communication promote openness and a common understanding of organizational priorities.Overall, a nonprofit budget can help businesses allocate resources and make decisions strategically, efficiently, and effectively.

Limitations of Zero-based Budgeting

Although there are many advantages of free budgeting, it also has some disadvantages:

1. Time and resource intensive: Adopting free budgeting can be difficult for businesses, when those who have a lot of work and very little are happy resources . Investigating and validating all expenses requires a significant investment of time and resources.

2. Complexity: It is difficult and difficult to implement a free budget, especially for large companies with many offices and cost centers. Extensive training and coordination may be required to ensure accuracy and consistency across the enterprise.

3. The main points: Time-to-time pricing leads to a short-term perspective and neglects long-term investments or strategic actions that are necessary for future growth, but may not produce immediate results.

4. Possible Bias: Project valuation or evaluation can influence the budgeting process, possibly misallocating resources or missing important costs.

5. Risk of Underfunding: Large projects or departments may not receive enough funding to reduce costs, which can negatively impact productivity and efficiency.

6. Back to change: The adoption and implementation of zero-based financing faces challenges due to backlash from employees accustomed to traditional financing methods.

7. Difficult to measure performance: It is difficult to assess the effectiveness of a non-profit fund with current performance indicators, it is difficult to assess its effectiveness and compliance impact on organizational culture and practices.

8. Inconsistencies in flow: The fact that budgets are created phase by phase results in a lack of continuity and consistency in resource allocation, making it difficult to assess long-term trends or compare performance. through the periods. Despite these shortcomings, non-financial budgeting is a useful tool for companies seeking to increase the efficiency, accountability, and strategic alignment of their budgeting processes. It's important to weigh the pros and cons and carefully evaluate whether a no-frills strategy is the best strategy for your company's needs and circumstances.

2.5.2 50/30/20 Budget

A well-known personal financial tip is the 50/30/20 budget, which proposes dividing your after-tax income into three categories:

1. Allocate 50% for Needs: This amount is allocated for necessities such as lodging, utilities, groceries, groceries, and the minimum amount owed on debt.

2. Demands at 30%: Discretionary expenditure on non-essential things like eating out, entertainment, vacation, hobbies, and luxuries falls under this category.

3. 20% for Debt Repayment and Savings: This amount is set aside for investments, savings, and overpayment of debt. It covers payments to retirement plans, emergency savings, and any overdraft debt repayment beyond the minimum.

By making sure they prioritize their requirements, indulge in certain wants, and save for the future, those who use this budgeting method can attain a healthy financial existence. But it's crucial to make adjustments based on unique situations and financial objectives.

Implementation of the 50/30/20 Budget

The 50/30/20 budget must be implemented in multiple steps:

1. Determine your total income after taxes: Add up all of your revenue from sources other than taxes, such as freelance work, regular payments, and other sources.

2. Identify your critical expenses: Enumerate all of your out-of-pocket costs, including rent or a mortgage, utilities, groceries, groceries, car insurance, and the bare minimum of debt payments.

3. Set Aside 50% for Needs: Determine how much of your post-tax revenue (after taxes) goes toward paying for necessities.

4. Set Aside 30% for Wants: Set aside thirty percent of your post-tax income for frivolous expenses such as entertainment, hobbies, dining out, etc.

5. Set Aside 20% for Savings and Debt Repayment: Determine how much of your take-home salary you have each month and set aside 20% for investments, savings, and debt repayment over the minimum. This covers extra debt repayment, retirement account contributions, and emergency savings.

6. Observe and modify: To make sure you're staying inside the budgetary constraints, keep a close eye on your expenditures. Adapt as necessary in light of shifting costs or income.

7. Prioritize savings and debt repayment: To attain long-term objectives and financial stability, concentrate on accumulating emergency and retirement savings as well as paying off high-interest debt.

Advantages of the 50/30/20 Budget

The 50/30/20 budgeting approach has a number of benefits.

1. Easiness: Even for individuals who are unfamiliar with budgeting, its simple format makes it simple to comprehend and put into practice.

2. Balanced approach: It encourages a balanced financial life by allocating cash to necessities, wants, savings, and debt repayment. This ensures that basic expenses are paid while still leaving room for discretionary spending and future savings.

3. Adaptability: The ratios are only recommendations; you can change them to suit your budget and unique situation. Customization based on priorities and personal preferences is made possible by this flexibility.

4. Encourages saves:By setting aside a sizable amount (20%) of income for debt repayment and savings, it helps people develop a savings attitude and accumulate emergency reserves, pay off debt more quickly, and save for long-term objectives like retirement.

5. A cognizance of finances: This budgeting technique necessitates frequent tracking of income and costs, which heightens awareness of spending patterns and facilitates the identification of areas that may require improvements.

6. Reduces financial stress: The 50/30/20 budget helps lessen financial stress and uncertainty by offering a clear plan for managing funds and reaching financial objectives. This can promote general well-being and peace of mind.

Limitations of the 50/30/20 Budget

Although the 50/30/20 budgeting approach offers benefits, there are certain drawbacks as well:

1. Using a universal strategy: Allotments may not be appropriate for all individuals. While those with smaller spending could feel limited by the 30% wants group, those with higher living expenses or substantial debt might

find it difficult to fit inside the 50% needs area.

2. Ignores individual situations: It doesn't take into consideration differences in family size, geography, income levels, or other unique factors that may have a big influence on priorities and spending demands.

3. Is not concerned about emergencies: Even while it sets aside 20% for debt repayment and savings, some people could find that this is insufficient to handle unforeseen costs or emergencies. It could be essential to have a separate emergency fund to deal with unforeseen expenses.

4. May not properly prioritize debt repayment: Although it sets aside some money for debt repayment, it doesn't give priority to high-interest debt or offer detailed instructions on how to pay off debt. For certain people, this could lead to ineffective debt payback.

5. Minimum investment guidance: Although it sets aside money for savings, it doesn't offer comprehensive advice on retirement planning or investment methods, which could restrict the possibilities for people looking to increase their assets over the long run.

6. Needs self-control and monitoring: Those who prefer a more hands-off approach to budgeting may find it difficult to maintain discipline and frequent tracking of costs necessary for the successful implementation of the 50/30/20 budget.

Overall, the 50/30/20 budgeting strategy can be a useful place to start when managing your finances, but it's important to understand its limitations and modify it based on your unique situation and financial objectives.

2.5.3 Envelope System Method

Using the envelope system budget, you set aside a certain amount of money for each category of spending, such as food, entertainment, and travel. You only use the funds in each envelope for the intended purpose, and each category has its own envelope. You cease making purchases in that category until the following budgetary month once the money in an envelope is empty. This approach facilitates efficient tracking and management of spending.

Implementation of Envelope System Method

Take these actions to put the envelope system budget into practice:

1. Identify Categories: List the major categories of your expenses, such as entertainment, groceries, utilities, and travel.

2. Assign Budget: Based on your income and expenses, allot a certain sum of money to each area. Make sure your overall allotment does not surpass your income by being sensible.

3. Acquire Envelopes or Containers: Get actual envelopes or containers for every area of expenditure. Give them appropriate labels.

4. Withdraw Cash: Take out of your bank account the specified sums of money for every category.

5. Fill the Envelopes: Using your budget allocations as a guide, put the right amount of cash into each envelope.

6. Monitor Expenditures: Utilize cash from the relevant envelope for each transaction you make. To make sure you stick to your spending limits in each category, keep a record of your purchases.

7. Replenish and Adjust: Review your spending at the start of each budgetary

period (such as weekly or monthly) and make any required adjustments to your allocations. Put the designated amounts for the new period back into the envelopes.

8. Adapt as Needed: Be adaptable and make adjustments to your budget as your financial circumstances change or you realize that you need to set aside more or less money in certain areas.

Advantages of Envelope System Method
The envelope system budget has a number of benefits.

1. Control and Awareness: By outlining precise spending caps for every category, it aids in improving your financial management. You get more awareness of where your money is going and are able to see potential areas of overspending.

2. Simplicity: The interface is uncomplicated and simple to comprehend. Tracking tools or complex software are not needed. Cash and envelopes are all you'll need.

3. Prevents Overspending: It automatically reduces impulsive or unnecessary purchases because you can only spend the amount in each envelope. You cannot spend more money in a category once it is empty; you must wait until the following budgetary month.

4. Encourages Saving: You can create a safety net by reallocating any money that is consistently left over at the end of each period to savings envelopes or debt repayment.

5. Reduces Debt: You can lessen your debt over time by managing your spending and setting priorities for where your money goes. This will make you less likely to rely on loans or credit cards to pay for bills.

6. Customizable: You are able to alter your categories and allotments to suit your personal priorities and financial objectives.

7. No Overdraft Fees: You won't run the risk of overdrawing your bank account and paying exorbitant overdraft fees because you're utilizing cash and only spending the amount you've set aside.

8. Encourages Communication: The envelope system promotes candid discussion about financial objectives and goals when budgeting with family or a spouse. In terms of spending decisions, it keeps everyone responsible and in agreement.

9. Adaptable to Varying Income: Since you're creating your budget based on your actual cash flow rather than counting on a steady salary, it might be very helpful for people or families with variable incomes.

10. Teaches Financial Discipline: The envelope method emphasizes the need of discipline and postponing gratification in managing finances by having users physically handle cash and make thoughtful decisions about how to divide it.

11. Aids in Recognizing Spending Trends: Tracking your expenses with the envelope approach will help you identify patterns in your spending habits over time. This information can assist you in modifying your spending plan and locating possible areas for more cost savings.

Limitations of Envelope System Method

The envelope system budget has several drawbacks in addition to its many benefits.

1. Inconvenience: Keeping track of cash for every transaction can be difficult, particularly in the digital age where most transactions are done online. For some expenses, carrying a lot of cash might not be prudent or safe.

2. Limited Tracking: Although the envelope method aids in keeping track of cash expenditures, it can miss certain costs if you occasionally make purchases with debit or credit cards. This may result in inaccurate financial records and make it more challenging to evaluate your financial status as a whole.

3. Risk of Loss or Theft: There is a chance that cash you carry could be lost or stolen. You risk losing the funds designated for those categories if your envelopes are misplaced or stolen, which could cause havoc with your budget.

4. Difficulty with Online Transactions: It can be difficult to use the envelope system for all expenses because some online transactions or bill payments call for a debit or credit card.

5. Lack of Rewards or features: Paying with cash prevents you from taking advantage of credit card features and rewards including cashback, travel rewards, and purchase protection.

6. Less Flexibility: Without modifying the budget, the strict cash distribution to designated categories of the envelope system may not be able to handle unforeseen costs or shifts in financial priorities.

7. Not Suitable for Everyone: Although the envelope system is effective for certain people or families, it might not be appropriate for everyone's financial status or way of life. Some people might find it harder to stick to a cash-only strategy or prefer digital budgeting tools.

2.5.4 Pay Yourself First Method

The "pay yourself first" method of budgeting involves prioritizing saving or investing a portion of your income before allocating money to other expenses. It emphasizes building savings or investments as a top financial priority. By consistently setting aside a percentage of income, individuals can ensure they're saving for future goals and emergencies before spending on discretionary items. It's often recommended to automate this process to make it easier to stick to the plan.

Implementation of Pay Yourself First Method

To apply the "pay yourself first" approach to budgeting, take the following actions:

1. Set Financial Goals: Decide on your short- and long-term financial objectives, such as emergency savings, retirement savings, or a significant purchase.

2. Get Savings As A Percentage: Prior to covering other expenses, choose a portion of your income to put toward savings or investments. 10%, 20%, or any other number that fits your budget and goals could be used here.

3. Automate Savings: Configure your checking account to automatically move funds to an investing or savings account. By doing this, you make sure that your savings are deposited before you have an opportunity to use them for other purposes.

4. Track Expenses: After saving, keep an eye on your expenditures to make sure you're still living within your means. Track your spending with budgeting tools or apps to find areas where you may make necessary cuts.

5. Modify as necessary: Make sure your savings and budget objectives still fit your priorities and financial status by reviewing them on a regular basis. To keep on course, make necessary adjustments to your spending or savings %.

6. Celebrate Milestones: To maintain motivation and strengthen sound financial practices, commemorate meeting savings benchmarks along the journey.

Advantages of Pay Yourself First Method

The "pay yourself first" method offers several advantages:

1. Prioritizes Savings: By automatically allocating a portion of your income to savings or investments before paying other expenses, it ensures that saving becomes a priority. This helps build a financial cushion for emergencies and long-term goals.

2. Consistent Saving: Automating savings makes it easier to stay consistent with your saving habits. Since the money is set aside before you have a chance to spend it, you're more likely to stick to your savings goals.

3. Reduces Financial Stress: Knowing that you're actively saving for future needs can reduce financial stress and provide peace of mind. It helps you feel more secure knowing that you have funds set aside for emergencies and future expenses.

4. Encourages Financial Discipline: The method encourages disciplined financial behavior by forcing you to live within your means after saving. It promotes conscious spending and can help curb impulsive purchases.

5. Facilitates Goal Achievement: By consistently saving towards your financial goals, whether it's buying a house, traveling, or retiring comfortably, you're more likely to achieve them. The method provides a structured approach to reaching your objectives.

6. Harnesses Compound Interest: By starting to save early and consistently, you can take advantage of the power of compound interest. Over time, your savings can grow significantly through interest and investment returns.

Limitations of Pay Yourself First Method

The "pay yourself first" approach to budgeting has several advantages, but it also has some drawbacks.

1. Potential Problems with Cash Flow: Cash flow issues may arise if you set aside a portion of your income for savings before covering other bills, particularly if your expenses are higher than your income. This could necessitate meticulous budgeting and perhaps modifying the savings percentage.

2. Dangers of Ignoring Required Expenses: Prioritizing savings over other costs, including rent, utilities, or debt payments, might have unintended consequences. Achieving a balance between urgent financial obligations and savings is crucial.

3. Hardness in Adapting: If your financial condition changes after the savings percentage has been automated, it could be difficult to modify it. For instance, you might need to temporarily lower your savings rate if you encounter unanticipated expenses or a drop in income, which could interfere with your long-term savings objectives.

4. Cost of Opportunity: While saving money is a good idea, devoting too much of your income to savings may cause you to miss out on opportunities to invest in your future self-worth or career advancement, such as professional or educational prospects.

5. The Possible Overuse of Automation If all you do is set up automated payments for savings, you might not be actively involved in managing your money. It's crucial to make sure your savings and budget are still in line with your financial goals by reviewing them on a regular basis.

6. Inflation Risk: Your funds may lose purchasing power over time if they are not invested in assets that grow faster than inflation. To protect the value of your funds, it is imperative that you think about investing in assets that provide returns higher than inflation.

7. Depletion of Emergency Funds: Even while the strategy promotes emergency savings, there are situations in which depending just on a set percentage may not be enough. Some crises, such as unexpected medical costs or job loss, can call for larger savings than the fixed % provides.

8. Variable Income Difficulties: It might be difficult to keep up a steady savings rate for people whose income is erratic or fluctuating, like commission-based employees or freelancers. Income fluctuations might necessitate modifying the savings plan, which would make automation more difficult.

9. A psychological component: Some people might find it challenging to put saving first when they have pressing needs or wants. For others, the psychological component of postponing satisfaction and giving long-term objectives precedence over immediate needs can be a hurdle.

10. The "One-Size-Fits-All" Method: The method's suggested allocation of a set percentage to savings might not be appropriate for every person's financial circumstances or aspirations. Since everyone has different financial responsibilities, objectives, and timetables, a more customized strategy to saving can be more appropriate.

11. Rates of Interest and Investing Hazards: Returns on savings can differ depending on where they are invested or deposited. The growth potential of savings could be restricted by low interest rates or high investment risks, which would reduce the method's efficacy in reaching long-term financial objectives.

12. Insufficient Adaptability: Automation has its uses, but it could not be flexible enough to change with opportunities or situations. A strict savings plan may make it more difficult to take advantage of advantageous financial circumstances or make adjustments for unforeseen costs.

2.5.5 The 80/20 Rule Budget

According to the Pareto principle, sometimes known as the 80/20 budgeting rule, 80% of your output should produce 80% of your returns. When creating a budget, allocate 80% of your income to savings and essentials like rent, groceries, and other fixed costs; the remaining 20% should be used for either savings or discretionary expenses like travel or hobbies. It's a manual that assists in setting sensible spending and saving priorities.

Implementation of 80/20 Rule Budget
The 80/20 budgeting rule must be put into practice in multiple steps:

1. Compute your income: Find out what your monthly gross income is after taxes.

2. Identify necessary expenses: Make a list of all the costs that you must pay, including your rent or mortgage, utilities, food, groceries, insurance, and debt payments.

3. Assign 80% of earnings: Set aside 80% of your salary for these necessities. This guarantees that you get the necessities and pay your payments on schedule.

4. Set aside 20% for non-essential items: The remaining 20% should be set aside for purposes like hobbies, entertainment, eating out, travel, and extra savings or used for discretionary spending.

5. Monitor and adjust: Keep tabs on your expenditures to make sure you're staying under your spending limit. Make necessary adjustments to account for variations in revenue or expenses.

6. Prioritize savings: Make saves for future objectives like emergencies, retirement, or big purchases your top priority within the 20% allotted for

non-essentials.

7. Exercise flexibility: The 80/20 rule is a useful structure, but it's not inflexible. Changes can be required depending on personal circumstances or financial objectives.

Advantages of 80/20 Rule Budget
The 80/20 budgeting rule has the following benefits:

1. Easiness: It offers a clear framework for distributing revenue, which facilitates the comprehension and use of budgeting.

2. Prioritization: It guarantees that basic needs are satisfied before discretionary expenditure by directing the majority of money towards necessary costs.

3. Emphasize essentials: Assists in determining and ranking necessary expenditures, guaranteeing timely payment of invoices and provision of necessities.

4. Flexibility: Gives freedom for enjoyment and the pursuit of personal objectives by allowing discretionary expenditure to be flexible.

5. Emphasis on savings: Within the 20% discretionary expenditure category, allocate a percentage of income to savings goals in order to highlight the significance of saving.

6. Goal-oriented: Promotes establishing and achieving financial objectives, such as debt repayment, vacation savings, or emergency fund building.

7. Financial awareness: Encourages frequent tracking of expenses and raises awareness of spending habits, which improves financial decision-making.

Limitations of 80/20 Rule Budget

The 80/20 budgeting rule has benefits, but it also has drawbacks.

1. Inflexible percentages: The set 80/20 split might not be appropriate for every person's financial objectives or circumstances. Some people could discover that they need to set aside more or less than 80% for discretionary or necessary expenses.

2. Lack of variability accounting: Since income and expenses might change from month to month, it can be difficult to always follow the 80/20 rule exactly.

3. Is not concerned with debt: The rule provides money for both discretionary and necessary spending, but it makes no mention of debt repayment plans, which some people may find to be of particular importance.

4. Reduced emphasis on saving: Although the rule sets aside 20% for savings and discretionary spending, people with high financial responsibilities or ambitious savings objectives may find that the regulation does not place enough emphasis on saving.

5. Is not concerned about emergencies: Because emergency reserves aren't specifically covered by the rule, people may be left vulnerable in the event of unforeseen costs or a loss of income.

6. Ignores individual needs: It might not take into consideration the many situations that each person faces, such as high housing costs, out-of-pocket medical bills, or expensive childcare costs, which might affect budgeting priorities.

7. May not support long-term objectives: Although the regulation promotes saving for objectives, people with long-term financial goals—like retirement savings or home ownership—might not have enough freedom under it.

3

Chapter 3

Saving Money Efficiently

3.1 Strategies for Saving Money

There are various methods for making savings:

1. Budgeting: Make a budget to keep track of your earnings and outlays so you may set aside money for savings.

2. Create savings objectives: To keep yourself motivated, decide what you want to save for and create precise, attainable goals.

3. Automate savings: To guarantee regular saving, set up automatic transfers from your checking account to your savings account.

4. Reduce wasteful spending: Examine your spending and find areas where you may make savings, such cutting back on eating out or terminating subscriptions that aren't being used.

5. Shop shrewdly: When buying purchases, search for discounts, evaluate costs, and use cashback or coupon applications.

6. Cook at home: If you want to cut costs on food, consider cooking your meals at home instead of going out to eat.

7. Refrain from impulsive purchases: Before making a choice, give purchases some thought and distinguish between needs and wants.

8. Save windfalls: Immediately transfer windfalls, such as bonuses or tax rebates, into savings.

9. Make use of cashback rewards: If your credit card offers cashback, use it to earn savings or statement credits.

10. Make sensible investments: To increase your savings over time, think about making investments in stocks, bonds, or real estate.

11. Emergency fund: Establish an emergency fund with the goal of covering three to six months' worth of living expenditures in order to handle unforeseen costs.

12. Bargain on bills: To save monthly costs, bargain for reduced prices on services like internet, cable, or insurance.

13. Do-it-yourself projects: To cut costs on professional service fees, take on do-it-yourself projects for home upkeep, repairs, or even personal grooming.

14. Take public transit: To save money on gas, parking, and auto maintenance, choose to take public transportation, carpool, bike, or walk instead of driving.

15. Energy efficiency: To reduce utility costs, use energy-saving techniques in your house, such as installing LED lighting, caulking cracks, and modifying thermostat settings.

16. Quantity buying: To take advantage of discounts and lower the cost

per unit, buy non-perishable things like cleaning supplies or toiletries in quantity.

17. Sell unneeded stuff: To get extra money, declutter your home and sell any unwanted or unused items through online marketplaces or garage sales.

18. Engage in conscious spending: To assist you prevent impulsive purchases, consider whether an item fits with your values and priorities before making it.

19. Handmade gifts: Rather than purchasing pricey products for special occasions, consider making homemade gifts to add a personal touch and save money.

20. Track your progress: Keep an eye on your savings to recognize accomplishments and maintain your will to save.

3.2 Building an Emergency Fund

Establishing an emergency fund is essential for both mental and financial stability. Here's a how-to manual to assist you in creating one:

1. Achieve a goal: Choose the amount of money you wish to put aside for an emergency fund. Aim for a minimum of three to six months' worth of living expenditures, which should include utilities, food, rent or a mortgage, insurance, and other living expenses.

2. Start small: If setting aside a sizable sum of money feels overwhelming, begin with a lesser amount and progressively raise it over time. Little things add up over time.

3. Make a budget: Examine your earnings and outlays to find areas where you can make savings and reduce spending. Make emergency fund savings a

top priority while creating your budget.

4. Automate savings: Establish regular, automated transfers, like once every payday, from your bank account to your emergency fund account. This makes sure you automatically contribute to your money on a regular basis.

5. Reduce expenses: Try to find methods to cut costs, such as going out to eat less, getting rid of subscriptions you don't use, or haggling for cheaper prices on things like insurance or cable. Put the money you save in your emergency fund instead.

6. Increase income: Look at ways to make more money, such as working a second job, doing freelance work, or selling things you no longer need. Boost your emergency savings with the additional funds.

7. Make use of windfalls: Rather than squandering unforeseen windfalls like tax returns, bonuses, or presents, put them straight into your emergency fund.

8. Remain focused: Defy the urge to divert your attention from your emergency fund aim in favor of spending it elsewhere. Remind yourself often of the significance of having financial stability.

9. Monitor your progress: Keep an eye on the amount in your emergency fund to determine how close you are to your target. Reward yourself for reaching milestones to keep yourself inspired.

10. Reevaluate and adjust: Make sure you're on track with your savings objectives by periodically reviewing your expenses and budget. As your financial circumstances change, make the necessary adjustments to your savings plan.

11. Make sensible use of windfall money: Refrain from overspending

whenever you get money that isn't expected, such as a tax refund or a gift. Rather, direct these windfalls straight into your emergency fund to hasten the process of saving.

12. Make sacrifices: To increase your savings rate, think about temporarily adjusting your lifestyle. You may, for instance, temporarily reduce your phone plan, forgo trips, or put off making large purchases until your emergency fund is completely replenished.

13. Start a side hustle: Look at ways to supplement your income by taking on freelance or side jobs. You can accomplish your goal more quickly if you allocate all of the additional money to your emergency fund.

14. Sell unused items: Sort through your belongings and get rid of anything you don't use or need. This could apply to furniture, collectibles, gadgets, clothes, or other items. Proceeds should be used to increase your emergency savings.

15. Review and change your goals: Check in with your emergency fund target and other financial goals on a regular basis. If something changes in your life, such a milestone you attain, think about modifying your savings goal.

16. Maintain it separate but accessible: Place your emergency money in a different savings account that you can quickly access in an emergency. Make sure it's not so close to hand, though, that you might be tempted to use it for non-emergencies.

17. Prioritize high-interest debt: If you have credit card debt or other high-interest debt, you should think about making payments on it a priority while you still make contributions to your emergency fund. You can transfer the funds you were spending to pay off debt to your emergency fund once your debt is under control.

18. Remain disciplined: Patience and discipline are needed to accumulate emergency savings. Remain committed to your objective even if it appears to be taking a while. Keep in mind that every dollar you save moves you closer to having a secure financial future.

19. Celebrate milestones: Celebrate each step you've taken toward your goals. Within your overarching objective, set smaller benchmarks and treat yourself when you meet them. This might support your motivation and attention while you save money.

20. Seek support: To stay accountable and motivated while you strive to accumulate your emergency fund, think about enlisting the help of a friend, relative, or financial counselor. Having a support system might help the process seem less overwhelming.

3.3 Automating Saving

By establishing automatic, weekly, or monthly transfers from your checking account to your savings account, you can automate your savings. Applications for opening bank accounts and managing finances with built-in automated savings features are also included. Using the circular service provided by certain banks or apps is an additional choice. Your credit card purchases are automatically rounded to the nearest dollar when you use these services, and the difference is transferred into your savings account.By the way, the following provides a thorough breakdown of how to automate your savings:

1. Establish clear objectives: Establish savings targets for any purpose, such as retirement, a house payment, a trip, or an emergency. You'll be better able to choose how much to save and why by setting clear goals.

2. Evaluate your finances: To ascertain your present financial status, carefully examine your income and expenses. Calculate the monthly amount that you

may securely save without going over your spending limit.

3. Create a Budget: Include goals for savings, expenditures, and income in your budget. Allocate a portion of your income for savings-related expenses.

4. Select the ideal account: Go for a savings account that offers enticing interest and minimal costs. High-yield savings accounts and certificates of deposit (CDs) are two options to consider if you want a larger return on your investment.

5. Configure the appropriate number: Locate the Transfer or Auto Pay area after logging into your online banking account or mobile app. Establish automated transfers between your savings and checking accounts. Indicate the frequency (weekly, fortnightly, monthly, etc.), start date, and transfer amount.

6. Have faith in direct deposit: If your employer offers cash, think about transferring a portion of your salary into a savings account. In this manner, you choose to reduce your expenditures.

7. Make use of tools and applications: Look at money management and budgeting apps with built-in automatic savings features. These programs can analyze your purchasing habits and automatically move money to your savings account based on pre-established rules or algorithms.

8. Consider Account Consolidation Services: You can use these services to round up your credit card purchases to the closest dollar and transfer the difference to your savings account. They are provided by certain banks and financial apps. Make numerous transactions with this option to improve your savings.

9. Check and Adjust: Evaluate your savings performance and make necessary adjustments to your automated savings plan. In reaction to price fluctuations

and inflation, think about raising your savings contributions.

10. Take a photo: Remain true to your savings plan in spite of distractions and unforeseen costs. Remember your long-term objectives and how crucial it is to provide your family with a safety net of money. You may automate the process and move closer to your financial objectives by adhering to these recommendations and keeping track of your saving behaviors.

11. Make Use of Apps That Save: Make use of specialized savings apps that move tiny sums of money from your checking account to your savings account on a regular basis. These apps frequently employ algorithms to examine your spending patterns and spot areas where you may save money.

12. Utilize Employer Initiatives: Find out if your company has any savings plans, like a 401(k) or other comparable auto-enrollment retirement plan. To optimize your savings, take advantage of employer-matching contributions.

13. Make Use of Cashback Rewards: If your credit card gives cashback, arrange for automatic redemption so that your savings account receives the cashback earnings. This makes it simple for you to save money and get incentives for your purchases.

14. Create Accounts Based on Goals: You can open several savings accounts with certain banks for various purposes, like school, travel, or a new car. To dedicate money toward particular goals, set up automatic transfers to these goal-based accounts.

15. Make Sensible Use of Windfalls: Automate some of your unexpected windfalls—such as tax returns, bonuses, or cash gifts—into your savings account and utilize the remaining amount for other financial objectives or spending. This guarantees that even in the event of unexpected financial gain, saving will always come first.

3.4 Importance of Emergency Saving

Preparing for emergencies is crucial for a variety of factors.

1. Emergency Fund: An emergency fund safeguards your funds by acting as a safety net to assist you in avoiding debt in the face of unforeseen expenses and challenging circumstances. Savings may become depleted or interest rates may become prohibitive over time.

2. Simplified Mindset: Anticipating and preparing for emergencies can alleviate the anxiety and tension that accompany an unstable economy. You will experience an enhanced sense of well-being by possessing a strategy to navigate unforeseen circumstances.

3. Pay off debt: Using an emergency fund prevents you from going into debt to cover unexpected expenses, such as medical bills or home or auto repairs. This will prevent the accumulation of debt with high interest rates, which can have detrimental effects on one's finances and complicate the process of making payments.

4. Maintaining Financial Independence: Being a safety net you can build your financial freedom on and avoid taking other people's help when you need it will be possible with an emergency savings fund. It gives you the ability to handle financial challenges without compromising your autonomy.

5. Protecting Long-Term Goals: Your reliance on emergency savings wouldn't exist, if you didn't save for the unexpected expenses, you'd have to consider withdrawing from your retirement savings or long-term savings. This can break your savings account that you need the most to reach your important financial goals, such as buying a property, funding children's education or early retirement.

6. Emergency Reserves: In the event of a job loss or other significant loss of

income, emergency reserves can provide short-term financial stability while you look for a new job or contemplate alternative sources of income. When facing the world and your own challenges, an emergency reserve is a great way to develop resilience, financial security and peace of mind. Building and maintaining an adequate emergency fund should be a top concern for anyone seeking to secure their financial future.

7. Protection Against Unexpected Events:People live unpredictably, and the chance of having an unexpected accident like natural disaster, accident, or serious illness are unavoidable which may occur at any time. Owning an emergency savings fund allows you to confront these unpredicted financial distresses without risking huge losses.

8. Quick Access to Funds: Liquid assets constitute a tangible part of one's emergency savings, as in a savings account or a money market account, readily available when required financially. As opposed to investments or retirement plans, which may be penalized or be unavailable for withdrawal, emergency savings can be withdrawn anytime as needed.

9. Flexible Solution for Various Expenses: The purpose of an Emergency fund is to cover a wide variety of expenses that may come up like health bills, home or car repairs, or deductibles for medical or home insurance, or on the job expenses. This is a perk that neither a traditional savings account nor a fixed plan like a term deposit or a long-term investment offers, and it ensures you are ready for any financial troubles that may unexpectedly arise.

10. Protecting Your Loved Ones: Emergency fund not only benefits you but also you become a good economist to your loved ones who can depend on you for financial support. Thereby you will certainly be able not to worry about such an issue since you are certain of the fact that your family's needs will be covered during times of hardship.

11. Reducing Stress on Relationships: Financial dilemmas will cause

tremendous tension in the marriage and bring about many disagreements. Emergency funds, projected by the savings, effectively protect your relationship from financial stress, thus enabling you to concentrate on bailing each other out at difficult times.

12. Opportunity to Seize Financial Opportunities: The point is that an emergency fund is a safety net that enables you to look for financial yields wherever you see the possibility. You can buy assets at discounted prices during market downturns, grab investment opportunities as they arise or go for career advancement that requires you to spend at least a portion up front.

Certainly, here are a few more reasons emphasizing the importance of emergency savings:Certainly, here are a few more reasons emphasizing the importance of emergency savings:

13. Protection Against Income Loss:Moreover, emergency savings can be utilized to cover during times of unexpected expenses, shortage or loss of work as in situations with reduced work hours, long leave without pay, or temporary layoffs. Savings is the function to let you pass the gap when wages are paid twice during a time.

14. Avoiding Financial Stressors: In other words, constant financial stress may result in a strong impact on mental and physical health issues. Through putting away emergency savings, you are in a position to handle financial hardship while catering to your personal welfare, which in turn encompasses a healthy lifestyle and good life.

15. Maintaining Creditworthiness: When an emergency fund is not accessible people tend to have to use credit cards or loans to take care of their sudden or unexpected expenses. Carrying out such expenditures may lead to a lot of indebtedness hence detracting from the credit score. Having emergency reserve funds is an important financial tool in this direction

because it enables you to postpone the use of credit to cope with the situations that have happened unexpectedly.

16. Preparing for Economic Downturns: For some people, it may affect job security, stability in finances , etc. Working as a shield, emergency savings provide financial stability and people can hold onto with a hope that those conditions will improve as time goes by.

17. Peace of Mind for Life Transitions: Lifelong transitions such as getting a family, changing careers and place of abode may create financial uncertainties in life. Having a reserve account for emergencies guarantees you peace whenever the change in employment settings comes, so that you cannot be dysfunctional because of the financial pressure.

18. Building Financial Discipline: Where the building and preservation of the emergency funds needs financial discipline and planning. You are able to build stable good savings and consistent fund contributions, which sustains you your whole financial life if you do this.

4

Chapter 4

Conscious Spending

4.1 Understanding Conscious Spending

E fficient spending means spending quite frugally. That is when you set aside a given sum of money and it should go for something that is really, really important to you and it is also a very good thing to meet your needs. It consists of a very meticulous process of making the mindful choices about the spending, tracking the expenses, and buying that delivers more than just principal value. But through this process of ethical spending, people avoid buying things without consideration for what they really want in their own life, which instead should match their own personal beliefs. It pursues a strategy that concentrates on the value of money as a self-expression so as to provide more continuity of one's financial life and also happiness. Furthermore, conscientious spending also encourages financial literacy as one's prudence becomes more apparent, paying attention to the direction where one's salary is going and how every cent can affect their general lifestyle. Targeted expenditure of resources makes informed spending a very powerful tool to many of the issues people face in their daily lives. It can help the people to find a deeper meaning in what they do and also ensure a financially secure future.

4.2 Identifying Needs vs. Wants

Here's a step-by-step guide to help you identify needs versus wants:

1. List Your Expenses: List everything you spend money on that you are aware of such as pay bills, buy food, go places, or do any leisure.

2. Prioritize Your Expenses: Classify your items on their importance and necessity. Start from the payables of the highest priority such as rent or mortgage, utilities and groceries.

3. Assess Survival Needs: List the places or items which must be reached immediately in order to secure your survival and existence. These basic needs are often the same and they are usually food, water, shelter, clothes and healthcare as well as transportation like to a work or a specialist visit.

4. Consider Safety and Security: Calculate costs connected to healthcare and safety as well as insurance (medicine and transport) and the amount of money you should allocate to emergency maintenance of your house.

5. Evaluate Health and Well-being: Identify the expenses that will be incurred by you for taking care of your health and wellness which will be inclusive of healthcare, medication, food that is balanced and exercise.

6. Differentiate Wants: Discuss the stuff or services that do not help the survival of man, but live a better life by him. The definition of this is the act of temporarily or permanently suspending the payment of certain debts. This may include eating out, entertainment subscriptions, expensive items and non-necessary traveling.

7. Assess Financial Impact: Think about how each expense will affect your

budget and how much you will have to reduce your spending in that area. Judge whether you will afford it consistently without risking your least important needs and money-saving projects.

8. Reflect on Long-Term Goals: Along with thinking of your long-term financial goals and aims, you also must take into account your financial priorities. Check if the things that finally got into your expenses list help you with the achievement of goals you have set, or shrink the amount of resources you have left.

9. Identify Trade-offs: Be aware that, possibly, in contrast with choices based on desires—certain giving up and compromises might be forced by prioritizing necessities. What expenses can you cut back or make a better fit with your present necessities and future objectives?

10. Regularly Review and Adjust: Check your expenditures and evaluate the difference between necessities and luxuries every now and then by taking into account the changing situation, your interests, and the financial status.

4.3 Mindful Spending Habits

One of the primary actions in learning how to practice mindful spending quotes intentionality and being conscious of just which channel your money travels to. Here are some tips to help you cultivate mindful spending habits:

1. Budgeting: Tally your expenses and income -that will be your start! Sort out your money on various categories like bills, foodstuffs, entertainment and saving. It is useful to check your budget to stay on track as sometimes things happen in life which may lead to a change of budget.

2. **Needs vs. Wants:Please distinguish between your requirements and your claim for them. The top priority must be food,shelter,and health,before the pleasure of spending on entertainment, or other accessories.

3. Avoid Impulse Buys: Stop and check yourself before buying anything with yourselves if it matches already to your beliefs. Do not enable yourself to sudden rush of purchases. This way you let yourself have the chance to think about whether you really need that thing or not.

4. Comparison Shopping: Research prices and options to check that you're not paying too much for some feature that only adds luxury to the car. Compare prices across vendors and prioritize used or even refurbished products in their choices where it is applicable.

5. Set Spending Limits: Put spending limits for each expense type to guide the budgeting process and avoid too much disbursement. Employ cash envelopes or digital applications to assist you in staying within limits for decisions on spending.

6. Track Your Expenses: Take into consideration what you spend and where so that you can see where you can save money and where you spend more unnecessarily. Make use of apps or spreadsheets for recording your transactions and review them periodically so as to recognize and work on the areas for further potential enhancement.

7. Practice Gratitude: Develop a mindset of gratitude based on what you have been given instead of being obsessed with having more things. Think over the purpose of the purchase and try to appreciate it even more.

8. Plan for the Future: Create and participate in a savings plan towards an ultimate goal, be it retirement, emergency, or key purchase, etc. Put your emergency fund first, and save for retirement second—these two goals will ensure your financial security in the long run.

9. Practice Delayed Gratification: Come to a decision as to the surveillance purposely help to also reduce the unintentional of the purchases. Setting your aspirations back would enable you to analyze whether the product is

what you want the most or your random flash of the moment. One action you will be doing patently is that your need to buy asymptotically approaches zero after allowing the heat to go down.

10. Use Cash More Often: Spending cash when shopping can make you feel it more and you will automatically think carefully about your own daily expenses. It may be very worthwhile to consider using the cash for such purchases, or having a separate cash budget for expenses on a monthly basis. Filling out this sheet can also help you to set limits on how much you spend in a day/week, and thus increase the awareness and conscious spending choices.

11. Unsubscribe from Temptations: Keep in mind that you must be as safe as possible when it comes to the exposure to the marketing and advertising that emphasize the frivolous consumption. If you no longer want to receive emails from a brand, subscribe to their list or search for them on social media. Use less energy by unsubscribing from the online shopping websites. Impulse spending sometimes happens without any alarm in this world of instant economic gratification. Thus, you can limit a lot of the unnecessary spending by removing the temptation and then direct your focus on your own important goals.

12. Practice Mindfulness: Try to make a pause before doing the impulse buy, then examine the need of the customer whether it is very much necessary. Think deeply about this question, and why do you value this item that's actually right for you based on your own aspirations and beliefs. The setting of the mindfulness practice may let you sense your own motivations better and also make your own sensible spending behaviors.

13. Set Financial Goals: Start by setting the realistic and also time-bound financial goals to frame your role in the spending. Whether it is saving a deposit for a lovely vacation, getting out of debt or purchasing a home, having a pointed direction of your spending can really help you to arrange your spending and also remain motivated, so you can make many good financial

choices.

14. Practice Contentment: Commit to contentment with everything you have today, and do not keep looking outward for more. Grant yourself a period to comprehend and appreciate what you have of possessions and experiences right now instead of always being desiring for the next purchase.

15. Engage in Regular Financial Check-Ins: To be more cognizant of your finances, block off a monthly hour or two to perform your due diligence. Try to check your spending patterns, settle on your financial goals, and make these possible either through tweaking your budget or your saving plans.

16. Consider the True Cost: Besides the financial implication, remember also the time, energy and sometimes, extended commitments that come after a purchase. Take into account if the thing is actually worthy in terms of its usefulness, the time it will last and the effect it may have over your health personally.

17. Practice Minimalism: Adjust to a simple living by considering the quality rather than the quantity of things you own and by continuously purging/eliminating useless objects. Instead of accepting raw materials, try to pay attention to experiences as well as relationships, and only keep the things which serve a purpose or bring you genuine joy.

18. Set Spending Challenges: Until you develop the skill to control the amount you are spending on specific areas, challenge yourself to reduce spending for a certain time. No matter how long you spend a month or a week, or how badly you go dry, setting up spending challenges help you become more aware of your spending manner and point out where it would be wiser to scrimp.

4.4 How to Avoid Impulse Purchases

1. Make a List: Making a shopping list ensures that you are concentrated on what is important and not on buying those things that you might not need, reducing the chances for impulse shopping. It allows you to focus on a specific shopping goal so that you do not have to get lost inside and quickly purchase anything that looks interesting. Respond to the following assignment topics and complete your work in a format that is clear, concise, and organized.

2. Set a Budget: Knowing the amount of money you've set aside for your budget enables you to sort out your expenses to ensure that you don't incur losses by purchasing on impulse. Be realistic and rational as per how far you can go and how much you can spend.

3. Wait Before Buying: The fact that you can stop a minute before buying something to see whether you just want it or it's a necessity helps you avoid unnecessary spending. Waiting for six months to a year helps people not give into impulse spending and wait for the right time to buy the most suitable thing.

4. Avoid Temptation: Identify the triggers and the reasons behind those impulsive shopping sprees and try your best to completely eliminate them. This could be done in various ways. A good example is declining subscriptions for marketing emails, not following brands tearing on social media or avoiding certain departments in the store.

5. Use Cash: Use cash instead of swiping credit/ debit cards. It will boost your willingness and awareness of spending. And when the money is actually being taken out of the wallet, the likelihood of you becoming hesitant before you decide on buying something is much higher.

6. Shop with Purpose: Shopping with a specific purpose of what to buy and

stuff to be killed decreases the chance of being tempted by impulse things. However, as the example of the grocery store, if you are just there to get the groceries, concentrate only on that and don't fall into the temptation of boredom and looking around other aisles.

7. Think About Value: Think about the fulfillment you will feel for the long-term use rather than simply its short-term appeal. Contemplate whether the particular item will make a meaningful difference in your life or if it's merely a frivolous gratification. Sample sentence: Specify the importance of taking the time to learn and understand how personal finances function.

8. Track Your Spending: Keeping track of your expenses becomes one of the most effective ways of identifying the pattern of your spending habits and the places where most of your impulsive dealing happens. Take advantage of spending apps or write down a simple finance plan by yourself.

9. Find Alternatives: Try to find other (cheaper) ways to fulfill your needs, but don't spend your money needlessly. For instance, if you need a book, which you have not read before, you can borrow one from the library or swap it with a friend, instead of going to a bookstore.

10. Practice Self-Control: Have you given thought at all to the financial goals you have set and the results of impulsive shopping? Be aware of your triggers and develop the techniques that help you to get through. For example, visualize, or reach out to friends and family. When you practice self-control, you will naturally form better spending habits as these evolve gradually.

11. Implement a Waiting Period: You rise up to this challenge by setting a personal rule, for example spending a specified amount of time between non-mainstream purchases. Putting some things on your wish list now and then gives you a chance to think and see the difference there is between what you just want to have and what you really need.

12. Unsubscribe from Retailer Emails: Email efforts of retailers are designed to lure you into buying when they have promotions, discounts, and other arrivals, putting you at the edge of only succumbing. Unsubscribe from these lists so that you will not be tempted to fall into the trap again and won't have to face the tempting promotions.

13. Practice Mindfulness: Be aware of your emotions and of things which can be triggering you while shopping. Take a moment and think about yourself why exactly it is that you feel like getting into an impulsive buying. Do you need help relieving stress, being passionate, or want some distraction? Addressing the source of these emotions is not just a way to cut off the head of the snake, but also a chance to have less impulsive spending habits.

14. Limit Exposure to Shopping Environments: Reduce the amount of time spent near locations that significantly raise the odds of making an impulse purchase, like malls, online marketplaces and certain shops. Contrary to that, change the way you spend your free time and don't do those things that are associated with shopping, for example, outdoor hobbies, exercise or friends' company.

4.5 Optimize Your Credit Cards

To optimize your credit card usage and minimize the risk of impulse purchases, consider these strategies:

1. Choose the Right Card: Pick a credit card that coincides with how you spend your money and your financial objectives. ch-5-incremental-innovation. Try to find just such cards with low interest rates, rewards programs that are appealing to you (such as cash back on groceries or travel rewards), and absence of maintenance charges.

2. Set Spending Limits: Set an appropriate monthly spending limit for your credit card as per the existing budget and the way your finances are doing. It

may prevent impulse purchases and thus, you can maintain a good budget for the expenses.

3. Use Auto-Pay: Do automatic payments for your credit card bill to make sure you never miss due dates and of course late fee payments. If you keep your balance at zero and strive constantly to avoid paying interest and build a good credit history at the same time.

4. Monitor Your Statements: While you should go about your credit card activities, be sure to periodically review your credit card statements to track your spending and identify any unauthorized or unusual charges. Hence, you will be conscious of your financial conditions and fraudulent areas, if any, as they crop up.

5. Utilize Alerts and Notifications: Activate the alerts and notifications shown by your credit card company in order to be conscious about your account activity. You can get a message when your purchases overspend a defined amount or your transaction expenses exceed to your specified threshold or around too close to a limit you had set. Notification is helping you to follow what you've planned and avoid impulse buying of any unnecessary item.

6. Opt-Out of Overdraft Protection: If the maximum and minimum amount in the credit card is too high thereby you may not be able to afford paying all the outstanding on time, consider reducing the clearing your outstanding credit card debt on time if your credit card offers overdraft protection, then decline this benefit. Utilizing overdraft protection enables your withdrawals to go through even when they exceed your credit limit with a high likelihood that your debt will increase and more fees will be due. With your decision to take the path of opting out, when you reach your credit limit, your purchases will be declined, stopping any prospect of you spending beyond what you can afford.

7. Use Virtual Credit Card Numbers: Certain credit card agencies have started to provide virtual credit card numbers aimed at online purchases. Temporary, one-time only, single-use-only, or time-bound numbers are tied to your account which are valid only for once or within a specific period of time. Virtual credit card numbering not only means users can have more secure transactions and less likely to be victimized by fraud but also lead to reduced identity theft.

8. Practice Self-Control: Consequently, while it is true that there is a great deal of freedom afforded with credit cards, it is important that self-control and mindful spending habits are used for the good of the credit card user. If you are thinking of buying something, just take a break first to reflect and examine whether that is really within your budget and financial goals. Once it's a detrimental purchase, you should allow time to vet it and check if it's prudent to have or not or if it can always wait.

9. Utilize Purchase Alerts: Most credit card companies provide purchase alerts of which you are notified via email or text message when transactions are spent with the card. Seize these alerts particularly to keep your expenses authentic and detect upcoming or costly transactions.

10. Review Rewards Programs: Take an overview of the credit card rewards from time to time to make sure you could take maximum benefits from them. Look for ways to achieve coupons by saving money on your outstanding balances, travels, or gift cards instead of using them to procure unneeded items.

4.6 Understanding Debt Management

Debt management is the solution-seeking exercise aimed to restore financial balance and ultimately escape from bad debt traps. This is an idea that involves introducing a detailed plan to repay debts in an organized approach so as to minimize the cost of default as well as thus interest while preventing default. It entails making a budget to designate money towards debt repayment as well as negotiating the interest rates of the loans or various figures so that the repayment time is extended and they are included by one single monthly fee. Through sticking with a debt management plan the people can regain control of their money, release the stress related to debt, and thus obtain a long-term financial health. Proper monitoring of debt demands forbearance, planning and generally, highly experienced involvement from a professional or credit advisory to tackle complex financial dilemmas.

4.7 Understanding Different Types of Debt

There are several types of debt, each with its own characteristics and implications:

1. Consumer Debt: These are the debts that are taken for the personal or family functions, to include the things such as credit card debts, personal loans, and also installment loans for a car or appliances.

2. Mortgage Debt: This type of debt service is very related to the purchase of a property. The term mortgages cover the many loans that usually have long payback terms and are covered by a security position in the property itself.

3. Student Loans: Borrowed money to help pay the college bills while acquiring the education in the form of tuition, books, and the living expenses. They can be public or they can be private and also be backed up by the government.

4. Auto Loans: These loans are often repaid over a very long time period, with the vehicle acting as security for the loan provider in case of default. As collateral property, a car is also very used to obtain auto loans.

5. Medical Debt: Accumulation of debt from medical bills, which include the hospital bills, doctor's fees, prescriptions, and even home health care.

6. Business Debt: Enumeration of the Earning of Income through Acquisition of Debt by the Businesses as a tool to finance the operations, purchase equipment or expand. This can be in the form of some credit facilities such as loans, lines of credit, or also bonds.

7. Payday Loans: Firstly, temporary, high-yield loans that are mostly employed to finance expenses whenever the borrower is waiting for their next salary. This is commonly known as the "mosquito breeding ground." They charge exorbitant fees and also interest rates.

8. Secured Debt: Assets that are used as back up, for example the house of car loan. The borrower who can't/can not accomplish the principal becomes the lender's headline of seizure of the collateral that helped the lender to meet the debt.

9. Unsecured Debt: Loans, which bear no guarantee or collateral. Installment plans or credit card and personal loans are common features. Lenders are concerned only about the creditworthiness of the borrower when it comes to assessment of his eligibility of the terms he is being provided.

10. Revolving Debt: Flexible credit line with a credit limit set to the predefined repayment structure so you can either borrow, pay, and borrow again and again. Credit cards are an important form of revolving debt and the finance industry is currently trying to withdraw people from the habit of using plastic money to pay for goods and services.

11. Installment Debt: The first thing a business loan agent typically wants to know is how much the business owner owes creditors, including the original loan amount, interest rates, and payback terms. In this group of installment credit lines, the mortgage, auto loans, and student loans are typical.

12. Government Debt: The debt was issued by governments at the national level, state and local authorities also participated in issuing debt to finance

public spending. The governing body issues bonds and treasury securities as the most paid forms of its debt.

4.8 Strategies for Managing Debts

Handling debts smartly means that you have to come up with strategies for reducing pressure caused by debts by replying to them on time. Here are some key strategies:

1. Create a Budget: Prepare a broad-based budget that shows all your income, expenditures, and loans payments. In your plan, budget a percentage of your payment towards reducing your debt obligations as well as your other basic living expenses and savings.

2. Prioritize Debts: Clearly identify between high-interest debts and the ones that are urgent for repayment at their deadlines and pay them first. It could be helpful to try focusing on the priority of paying off debts with the highest interest rates first, or make smaller ones first and gain quick wins (the debt avalanche method or the debt snowball method).

3. Negotiate with Creditors: Make a move by contacting creditors in order to prompt them to maintain low interest rates, lower dues or extend repayment duration. The willingness of many creditors to engage with indebted people who encounter financial difficulty to find mutually beneficial solutions has been duly noted.

4. Consolidate Debts: Combine several loans into one with the lower interest and all payments may be made in one place thus reducing the total interest that you are charged. Different consolidation choices, for example, balance transfer credit cards, debt consolidation loans and home equity loans, could all lead to the same end result.

5. Increase Income: Target to generate more income from part-time jobs

or freelancing, search for better-paying jobs, and consider getting yourself a co-job or part-time job. By allocating a part of the extra income to debt repayments, there is an opportunity to clear all debts faster, which will thereby relieve some financial pressure.

6. Cut Expenses: Highlight the places you can make your impulse spending shrink and use this money opportunity to replenish your debts. Try to cut expenses such as memberships and gym visits, or even bargain for better offers on your bills.

7. Seek Financial Counseling: Communicate with a financial specialist or counselor for customized recommendations about dealing with your debts, budgeting, and shaping your financial behavior. They can offer good tips and experience of wise practical steps, and assist in the maze of troubling financial matters.

8. Automate Payments: To avoid arriving late with a payment deadline, it is advisable that you set up an automatic payment plan for your debts. This will enable you to be aware of when next payments are due, the total amount that is owed, and help you make regular progress to financing down.

9. Utilize Windfalls and Bonuses: Use unexpected windfalls, like overpaying taxes, earning a bonus or bequeathment, toward the debt repayment. A lump sum payment that goes toward either additional payments of an existing debt or full debt payment within a short time will accelerate your overall debt payment timetable.

10. Stay Organized: Be very thorough with your debts; monitor and track all payments and their schedules, with the aim of reaching closure. Exploit applications such as spreadsheets, debt payoff calculators (or debt tracking apps) which would help you keep your financial status in check and also stay inspired.

11. Build an Emergency Fund: Having a reputation for an emergency fund, check of unanticipated expenditures, will help avoid credit cards or loans for covering the utility bills. Subsequently the philosophy of compulsory saving at least 3 to 6 months of living costs in a quick-reach commission.

12. Avoid Taking on New Debt: Overcome the prospects to acquire new debts in your current effort for repaying existing debts. Picking out the necessities and resisting from incurring debts is a significant requisite towards the avoidance of excess indebtedness.

13. Monitor Credit Report: It is advisable to check your credit report after every six months so as to look out for any mistakes that might have been made and take corrective action where necessary. Refuting inaccurate critical information immediately preserves or ameliorates your credit score in the future.

14. Seek Support: Being shy of asking your friends and family for help is not good for your debt management if you are crippled by this. So it will be helpful if you seek their advice or support at these lines of difficulties. It can make a difference to talk to others concerning the hardships you encounter and achievements in paying off your debt. A person can acquire much-needed emotional support and encouragement that aids in such a difficult journey.

Certainly! Here are additional tips for avoiding common debt traps: Here are additional tips for avoiding the common debt traps:

9. Living Within Means: Even most pleasurable activities or hobbies fall short in the value compared to the financial freedom that traveling affords us. Try your very best not to overspend, in order to prevent it from leading you to unnecessary debts.

10. Negotiating Lower Rates: It is also very important to consider the ways to obtain discounted interest rates on the current debts, such as the bank or

credit card loans, which will save you the interest later on.

11.Regularly Reviewing Finances: Try and take a quick session at least every month or two to find out how your financial condition is doing in terms of income, expenses, and also debts. Contemporize your tactics as the progression of the events demand and strive not to lose sight of what you wanted to achieve from the financial goal.

12. Building Credit Wisely: Embrace credit prudently to build a prosperous credit history, but also mind to stay away from excessive debts you get from it only for the purpose of increasing your credit score.

13. Setting Financial Goals: Zero in on the specific strategic financial objectives, for example reducing debts, preparing for retirement, or saving dollars set aside for emergencies and act consistently with such goals.

14. Avoiding Payday Loans: Better to be clear of the payday lending and other high-cost and also short time revolving fees which often come with impossibly high rates of interest and charges that can make things a lot worse especially for someone who is a poor borrower.

15. Seeking Support When Needed: It's not a crime to ask for help when you're having trouble with debt management. Talk with a financial advisor, a credit counselor, or a friend or family member if you need it. Sometimes, still a point of view coming from outside could be very beneficial to get insight and direction.

16. Staying Organized: Monitor your financial accountabilities very closely, and keep records of pending payments and your payment schedules that will help you to avoid late payment fees, further interests, and penalties that can really aggravate your debt problems.

17. Practicing Patience: Understand that the search for financial stability

and the process of repaying the debts are not immediate or spontaneous but require your persistence. Keep calm and keep committed to the financial ladder staircase.

5

Chapter 5

Increasing Income Streams

5.1 Understanding multiple income streams

The whole notion of the alternative income streams revolves around finding the sources other than a bedrock job to make the money. Examples of these streams of income may be rental properties of your own, dividends from the investments you are making, income from your works of creativity such as royalties as well as income from side businesses you have created or jobs you do on a freelance basis like affiliate marketing and so forth. Diversifying the sources from which our income is drawn mitigates the risks and also ensures steady financial flow even in the shaky conditions of a market economy. It is also a great way for the employers to save on the labor costs and can greatly increase the number of earnings which might greatly affect the income of the people. This is because unlike in a situation where one would be entirely dependent on only one source of income, the individuals who have created the different income streams will already have a cushion of security which prevents a single event from completely ruining their financial position. This is why diversifying the income streams is not only a risk management strategy but is very inspiring and also rewarding as well, encouraging different goals and also allowing to build wealth over the period of time. Generating from several revenue sources at the same time is indeed an very important element in being a financially secure and also independent individual.

5.2 Types of Income

1. Earnings: Cash obtained by diligence. Usually, commissions, fees, tips, or bonuses that you get for your labor are where this money originates from. This is the primary source of income for the majority of people and frequently involves a regular wage.

2. Intermediate Income: Passive income is the result of investments or assets that need little upkeep. revenue from real estate, bonds, savings accounts, equities, mutual funds, and income from intellectual property like music, books, and some model patents.

3. Income Fraction: This kind of income is given by income. This includes income from real estate holdings, dividends from stocks, interest from bonds and savings accounts, and capital gains from the sale of investments.

4. Royalties: When their creations are used, owners of intellectual property may be paid royalties. This can include royalties that artists receive for licensed artwork, fees that writers receive for book sales, payments that composers receive for streaming or downloading their music, and fees that producers receive for copyrights.

5. Side Hustles: This is an extra revenue stream from a part-time employment in addition to your primary position. This can involve working as a freelancer in a range of fields, including consulting, writing, and graphic design. It may also refer to the online sale of goods. operating a vehicle for ride-sharing companies; managing an Airbnb listing.

6. Business Income: This is the money derived from owning and running a business. The sale of products or services, advertising fees, revenue from advertisements, affiliate marketing, etc., can all contribute to this. Investing in your business or partnering with it might also benefit investors.

7. Affiliate Marketing: Affiliate marketing is promoting other companies' goods and services in exchange for a fee that you receive for each sale or recommendation that comes about as a consequence of your work. This can be accomplished through blog postings, social media, email marketing, and other internet platforms.

8. Earnings and Interest: You receive interest when you lend money to a bank or another lender. Savings accounts, bonds, and certificates of deposit (CDs) are typically used for this. Investing in stocks of businesses that distribute profits to their shareholders yields dividend income.Benefits, obstacles, and opportunities exist for every kind of revenue stream. People can strengthen their financial basis by spreading their income from these several sources.

9. Buying and Selling Real Estate: Purchasing a home, making improvements, and then reselling it for a profit are all profitable endeavors. This holds true for residential homes, business structures, and even undeveloped property.

10. Online Courses and Workshops: Create and instruct online courses or workshops on subjects you are enthusiastic about to make a steady income. Websites like Teachable, Skillshare, and Udemy make it simple to reach a wide audience.

11. E-Commerce: Setting up an internet store to sell goods is either the only or the only profitable business strategy. Selling your goods at a discount, purchasing from a wholesaler, or producing them yourself are your three possibilities.

12. Peer-to-peer Lending: People can lend money to one another on websites

like LendingClub and Prosper and get a return on their investment.

13. Creating Materials: Producing content for podcasts, YouTube, TikTok, and other websites can bring in money. Selling goods, advertising, sponsorships, memberships, and other activities can also bring in money.

14. Images and Stock Images: Creative professionals can sell their images, movies, or photos to websites such as Shutterstock, Adobe Stock, or Getty Images, and earn free money.

15. Interaction and Training: You can get money from your expertise by providing consulting or training services in your field.

16. Description: Purchasing a franchise allows you to take use of a business plan and a brand. A broad range of industries, including food, retail, hospitality, and education, offer marketing opportunities.

17. Real Estate Investment Trust (REIT): Real estate benefits can be obtained without the burden of management by investing in REITs. Income-producing properties are owned and managed by REITs, which distribute a portion of their earnings to investors.

18. Peer-to-peer Sharing Economy: Use platforms like Turo, Airbnb, or Neighbor to rent out assets like cars, motorbikes, appliances, or parking spaces to make money with little work at all.

19. Mobile Apps: Tech-savvy business owners can develop and monetize mobile apps with in-app purchases, advertising, or subscription services to generate a passive income stream.

20. Cryptocurrency Mining and Investing: These activities can be extremely profitable, but they are also riskier and more volatile.People can raise their income and achieve financial independence by using these extra techniques

for earning numerous incomes.

5.3 Importance of Multiple Income Streams

It is crucial to afterall keep in mind that being well-off financially may also give you a certain level of comfort, flexibility, and support to life uncertainty. Here's why:

1. Risk Reduction: We engage in various actions that expose us to the possibility of sudden and unexpected income loss from the major source of income if we depend on only one income source, for example job, we are prone to job loss due to factors such as job losses, economic crises, or industry disruptions. Through diversification of sources of income, riskiness of the sources is reduced and exposure to unprecedented circumstances and events is minimized to a certain level.

2. Stability and Consistency: Multiple sources of income can not only provide one with a much more stable and consistent source of income compared to relying on just one pay cheque but it can also lessen the impact of the financial shocks and weather economic downturns. Even if the distribution pattern of customers across the streams evolves from time to time, there are still very many trends that may not be affected, it actually brings financial stability.

3. Financial Flexibility: A multi-source revenue stream (including a paycheck, share market, or an investment) gives you various options for spending, investing, or saving and provides you with much more flexibility than a single source of income. Apart from being a catalytic element for realizing the lifetime's dreams, it can also give the individuals an edge to pursue opportunities that have hitherto been a financial burden.

4. Increased Earning Potential: Diversification of the income stream can raise the totality of the income flow by going for the assets producing alternative

revenue. Each platform may have a different growth possibility. As a result, one person can optimize their own earnings and have a better chance of achieving their own financial goals faster.

5. Resilience in Economic Uncertainty: In a situation of a recession or market volatility, being inclusive in the several streams of income you possess, can help to overcome the financial turbulences. This enables the users to adapt to new situations as well as to continue with financial resilience in even the most challenging moments.

6. Long-Term Wealth Building: You can supplement and put much more emphasis on saving for the long-term by including more than one income stream. The people get the opportunity to do that when they diversify the investments, earn passive income and also explore entrepreneurial investment as well. Through these avenues, people can build wealth over the span of time and secure a better future for themselves and their families.

7. Emergency Preparedness: Multiple income streams are, in fact, a financial insurance, and can be particularly useful for the bad times, e.g. during emergencies or unforeseen expenses. It gives the role of being able to give relief to individuals and make them stay away from debt or save up resulting in many unexpected changes.

8. Diversification of Skills and Talents: The process of the exploration of the variety of income streams allows the individual to increase all realms of self including skills and talents, professional expertise, and overall personal growth. This diversity enables a product to be sold to a larger market but it also makes a career path and the sense of accomplishment available.

9. Lifestyle Design: The advantages of multiple income streams consist of their capacity to expand the horizon and offer an opportunity to line up the lifestyle according to personal goals and priorities. Whether it's a hobby, pursuing a dream, traveling, or having more time to spend with relatives,

differing revenue streams might as well give the financial backing needed to support a desirable way of life.

10. Retirement Planning: Having multiple streams of income should be included in the retirement plan, which is of great importance that company pensions plans have been getting fewer. The people who are able to form passive income like investment, rental properties, trademarks, and more will be able to sustainably live during the after-retirement years because the income will continue to flow and would lead to a comfortable living.

11. Legacy Building: Generating multiple streams of income can help building a legacy not only by accumulating savings for the next generations but also by creating value and encouraging unit contribution. Their support is not merely limited to providing for their family members but it extends to their future generations through having a financial plan that supports a philanthropic cause or charity.

12. Entrepreneurial Spirit: Creating an income stream may mean even more for people because it is freeing of the mindset of the entrepreneur wanting to be creative in different spheres. It makes one explore new opportunities, take calculated risk, and start to innovate in various areas. The fact that business owners must be able to take calculated risks and be innovative and adaptive to market changes is testimony to the high values of resilience, resourcefulness and creativity that are seen as desirable in today's economy.

13. Psychological Well-being: Diversifying the sources of income can be very beneficial toward getting better psychological health for relaxing from financial stress and for confidence about a better future. Having in mind that a solid foundation in income secured by more than one income source gives a feeling of stability and self-confidence, it promotes more leisure and wellbeing, the aspects people need to remain happy.

14. Adaptation to Technological Changes: Nowadays in the environment of

fast-moving technological revolution, multiple income avenues have a huge advantage in that they help people change their jobs force and adjust to the new industries and trends. A variety of income resources can lead to more people taking the advantage of the transition from traditional ways of doing business into digital platforms, to marketing and to the opportunity to do remote work as well.

15. Geographical Independence: As more and more people find themselves in the position of either working remotely or becoming digital nomads, having a variety of income streams offers workers the freedom to work or travel to anywhere on the planet. This geographical independence helps people gain access to lower living costs, discover new cultures and have their lightest lifestyle dreams without considering the responsibilities of wages and career advancement.

16. Resilience Against Inflation: Inflation eats into the spending power of money over time, and as a result, constant income needs to either keep up with inflation or a significant level of outsmarting it. Diversifying income sources, especially the ones linked to the investment like stocks, real estate, or commodities will result in keeping the assets value that is protected from the inflation world, and this will preserve the money in the long run.

17. Tax Efficiency: Strategic structuring of income streams is the best way to help being tax efficient and the reduction of the taxes amount. With income diversification across different sources and use of tax deductions, credits and proper investment vehicles like 401(k) or Roth IRA which offer tax benefits the individuals can opt for maximizing post tax income and thus preserving more of the earnings.

5.4 Strategies for Increasing Income Streams

The following are some methods for boosting revenue streams:

1. Identify Marketable Skills: Evaluate your abilities, know-how, and proficiency to determine what areas you can provide to others. This could include talents that others are willing to pay for, interests, hobbies, and skills relevant to your line of work.

2. Start a Side Business: Depending on your abilities, passions, or market need, start a side business or entrepreneurial endeavor. This could be making and selling goods, providing services, or making money off of a passion project or pastime.

3. Invest in Education and Training: To improve your abilities and credentials, make an investment in more education, training courses, or certificates. This can boost your earning potential and create new avenues for freelance or higher-paying employment.

4. Explore Passive money Opportunities : Seek out options that yield money with little to no continuing work, such investing in real estate, stocks, or bonds, or developing digital goods like software, e-books, or online courses.

5. Make Money Off of Your Assets: Determine which of your possessions, such as rental homes, cars, equipment, or intellectual property like books, music, or photos, can be sold. Try to find ways to sell, lease, rent, or obtain a license for these assets in order to make money.

6. Optimize Current revenue Streams: Examine your current sources of revenue and consider how you may increase and optimize your profits. This could entail raising prices, gaining more clients, increasing productivity, or broadening your product line.

7. Freelance or Consulting Work: In your area of expertise, make yourself available as a freelancer or consultant. This enables you to take advantage of your abilities and background to offer clients beneficial services on a flexible schedule, frequently at a greater cost than in a regular job.

8. Create Multiple Streams inside Your Industry: Look at other options within your sector to generate extra revenue. This could entail partnering with companies that complement one another, focusing on new markets or client segments, or providing alternative services.

9. Create an Online Presence: Use websites, blogs, and social media to create an online presence that highlights your abilities, knowledge, and services. This may draw in clients, consumers, or chances for product sales, consultancy engagements, or freelancing.

10. Network and Collaborate: Make connections with experts in your field as well as possible partners, customers, or clients. Developing connections and alliances can open up new doors for you in terms of collaborations, recommendations, and new revenue streams.

11. Diversify revenue Sources: To reduce risk and boost stability, diversify your sources of revenue. Investigate several revenue streams, such as jobs, freelancing, investments, rental properties, and passive income opportunities, rather than depending solely on one.

12. Remain Adaptive and Agile: Keep yourself updated on market trends, business advancements, and new opportunities. Be flexible and ready to change course when necessary to take advantage of new possibilities or adjust to shifting market conditions in your revenue strategy.

13. Utilize Online Marketplaces: Take advantage of online marketplaces like Etsy, eBay, Amazon, or Shopify to sell products or services. Enjoy the advantage of 21st century technology connecting the world. The sites are a

stage to a huge customer market and can be a successful way of making your crafts, creations or other kinds of specialties.

14. Monetize Your Expertise: Present consulting, coaching and e-learning webinars based on your professional career experience. Feed your inner wisdom, stories, and mentorial guidance to those who are fancy ready to pay for custom made assistance.

15. Affiliate Marketing: Team up with companies and businesses whom you should be able to effectively promote their products or services. Therefore, any commissions that result from sales or referrals through your marketing endeavors will be given to you. This can be achieved in many ways such as bar blogs, social media, email marketing, or any online channel.

16. Participate in the Gig Economy: By doing side work through platforms like TaskRabbit, Uber, Lyft or Upwork you can pay for extra money on an all at-your-own time basis. From a freelance graphic designer to a driver of an Uber car or an independent contractor, these platforms bring all of these options to one place.

17. Leverage Your Network: Utilize the contacts available within your reach by networking with colleagues, relations, friends and family and you are likely to identify potential clients and customers alike. Your referrals will eventually develop into partnerships that will enable you to expand your revenue channels.

18. Create and Sell Digital Products: Create digital products like e-books, templates, workbooks, or software applications that can help alleviate issues or solve problems faced by your target groups. Take your products online by selling them on your website, online platforms or digital shops.

19. Generate Passive Income through Royalties: Compose intellectual property like books, music, artworks or images, and, when your products

are sold or used, you may be paid royalties. Get acquainted with publishing companies, licensing agencies, online stores or any other types of exhibition, which will help you represent your work.

5.5 Practical Tips for Implementation

5.5.1 Setting SMART Goals

A highly useful tool for making it easier to create enumerable goals that are precise, understandable, practical, appropriate, and planned is the use of SMART goals. An explanation of each part is provided below: Below is an explanation of each and every element:

1. Specific: Objectives must be well-defined and unambiguous. If they are formulated in this manner, they will be attainable. They must provide answers to the following queries: How can I fulfill my dream? Why, therefore, is this purpose absolutely necessary? Who takes part? Where should it take place, exactly?What materials are required?

2. Measurable: In order to track and evaluate the progress track, targets and success indicators must be quantifiable. They ought to respond to queries like: Will we keep bleeding ourselves to death or find a cure?In what number? How am I going to know when they're reached?

3. Achievable: The objectives must be strategic, voluntary, and compatible with your limitations, abilities, and resource base. They should respect your personal space while staying within the bounds of reality. However, with sufficient time and effort, you will achieve your own objective.

4. Relevant: Your long-term objectives and your numerous life priorities should be tightly related to each other. They ought to be crucial to your identity and to your goals in life, work, or company. Hence the essay is available for a very low price.

5. Time-bound: It is vitally important to take into account the deadline or due date for each goal. It increases your level of excitement and gives you the drive to support your commitment. It provides an answer to the query: When do I receive the necessary mentorship?

Setting SMART goals is one approach to go about it. These goals create a path that is specific to the task at hand, as well as a means of gauging your own progress in an approachable, timely, and relevant manner. It helps you stay focused and accountable for your objective by framing your goals in a black-and-white way, which considerably increases your resilience.

How to set Smart Goals

SMART goals setting needs to be carried out through a guideline process which involves the defining of objectives that are Specific, Measureable, Attainable, Relevant, and Time-bound.Here's a step-by-step guide:

1. Identify Your Goal: Start with the target you want to achieve. It can be the increasing of the traffic to our site or it can be the growth of brand awareness. Define your target and be sure what the objective is, why you need it and what is significant.

2. Make it Specific: Provide more clarification concerning your purpose to ensure it is precise and to the point. Clearly indicate what you stand to achieve, those engaged and the venue as well as others that need to be included.

3. Ensure it's Measurable: Set up for rating progress and victory as indicators. Determine thoroughly how you will be monitoring your triumph and at what point the goal is succeeded. Establish which goal indicators you may use to ascertain just how far you have achieved your goals.

4. Make it Achievable: Assessment of how practical and achievable the goal is given the available resources, skills as well as other constraints. Think

about what is the best way to work on achieving your goal and how you can get certain resources and support for that.

5. Ensure it's Relevant: Double-check that the goal is consistent with yours and your goals along with your values, principles and objectives. Explore how the target aspires to be and in what way this target is integrated in your life template. This template could be the one of your life, career or business.

6. Make it Time-bound: Set the deadline or time frame of when you want the goal to be accomplished. By establishing a definite deadline, you will have a sense of running the clock and thus it will be easy to keep up the pace and persistence. Set a clear timeframe when you want to accomplish the goal and give yourself – milestones on the way.

7. Write it Down: Once you have specified your SMART goal, put it as a precise statement in black and white or as a plain text. Mention everything that needs to be mentioned and include all the criteria for the success of these initiatives.

8. Create an Action Plan: Consider your goal piece by piece, rather than treating it as a very massive and insurmountable barrier. Identify the actions that you have to take to move the goal put forward at the top and set a deadline for the completion of each step.

9. Track Your Progress: Monitor your goal every once in a while and don't get worried if you are not reaching it yet. Track your performance by keeping details about your actions, achievements, and also difficulties and conflicts that you confront during the entire process.

10. Adjust as Needed: Be a flexible thinker who is willing to correct his or her way if the need arises. If facing any challenges or any external forces alter your objective, reconsider your target and develop some appropriate manipulations to your action plan.

Through doing this, you will be able to set many SMART goals that are precise, measurable, ambitious but attainable, relevant and also detailed with a deadline. The result will be increased odds of achieving the set objectives with much higher focus and motivation.

5.5.2 Time Management and Prioritization

1. Time Audit: To monitor how you're currently spending your time, do a time audit. For a week or two, keep a thorough journal of everything you do to see trends, time wasters, and places where you may be more productive.

2. ABC technique: Set task priorities according to the ABC technique, where activities in A are the most crucial, tasks in B are less urgent but still vital, and tasks in C are optional but pleasant to have. Prioritize finishing your A tasks before tackling your B and C projects.

3. Eat That Frog: Made famous by Brian Tracy, this idea advocates taking on your hardest or most despised duty first thing in the morning. Gaining momentum and a sense of achievement by "eating the frog" early will carry over into the remainder of the day.

4. Temporal Blocking Strategies: Try out various time blocking strategies, including the 52/17 method (work for 52 minutes, then take a break for 17 minutes) or the 90-minute work cycle (work for 90 minutes at a high level, then take a longer break). Choose a technique that maximizes your energy and productivity.

5. The Two-Minute Rule: This states that you should do a task right away if it takes less than two minutes. This keeps little things from stacking up and getting too much on your plate, which frees up your mind for bigger, more crucial chores.

6. Priority Matrix: Sort jobs according to their importance and urgency in a

priority matrix or grid. You may rapidly determine which chores to assign or postpone and which to concentrate on with the aid of this visual tool.

7. Time Management applications and Tools: Find out how to track time, create reminders, organize projects, and assess productivity with these and other time management applications and tools. RescueTime, Asana, Trello, and Todoist are a few of the well-liked choices.

8. Batching Tasks: To reduce context switching and increase productivity, group related tasks together and finish them in batches. Establish designated periods, for instance, for answering calls, checking emails, or working on particular tasks.

9. Mindfulness and Focus Techniques: To train your attention and lessen distractions, practice mindfulness and focus techniques like meditation, deep breathing exercises, or the Pomodoro Technique.

10. Daily and Weekly Planning: Schedule time to organize and rank your responsibilities at the start of each day and each week. Review your objectives, plan your most critical tasks, and establish reasonable expectations for your ability to do them during this period.

11. Running Time Matrix: This matrix, which divides tasks into four categories based on importance and speed, belongs to Stephen. Covey's "7 Habits of Highly Effective People." Category 1 is important but not urgent, category 2 is important but not urgent, category 3 is important but not urgent, category 4 is not important, it is urgent. Instead of focusing on urgent tasks in Phase 1, set tasks in Phase 2 to address tasks that are important but not urgent.

12. Cool Time: How to do it: Practice time management by assigning specific tasks or tasks to defined blocks of time on your calendar. This will ensure that you have enough time for each task and prevent vulnerabilities from

releasing your product. Try using multiple time slots for different activities: meetings, deep work sessions, email management, breaks, etc.

13. Goal Setting: Make sure your daily responsibilities and tasks are aligned with your priorities and goals. Review your daily activities to see if they are helping you reach your goals. Think about whether the tasks you're completing are bringing you closer to your goals or distracting you from your higher-level goals.

14. Parkinson's Law: According to Parkinson's Law, employees will increase to stay at the appointed time to complete. To avoid this situation, set deadlines for virtual projects to stimulate enthusiasm and prevent procrastination. Setting deadlines can improve your productivity, focus and avoid unnecessary procrastination.

15. Thought Exchange Protocol: Establishes protocols that mark the beginning and end of periods of focused work. By mentally switching between activities or tasks, these routines can increase focus and productivity. Stretching exercises, deep breathing, writing, and reviewing priorities and goals are examples of transition techniques.

16. Continuous Improvement: Develop a mindset of continuous improvement in basic management skills and time. To increase productivity, review your workflow regularly, look for weak points and gaps, and try new methods. Think about what works and what could be better, and be willing to change your strategy as needed.

17. Adaptation and Flexibility: Being flexible and adaptable to unexpected changes or interruptions is important as a creative way of managing time. Learn to change course quickly when priorities change and be prepared to adjust your plans and schedules to take advantage of new opportunities or situations.

18. Self-Care and Life: Self-care and wellness are important aspects of time management. To replenish your energy and maintain your physical and mental health, schedule time for rest, relaxation, exercise, and recreation. Remember that maintaining a work-life balance is necessary to remain productive.These additional time management and prioritization skills will help you achieve your goals and manage your time better, making you more productive in your daily life.

Through the application of these more profound time management and prioritization techniques, you can improve your efficiency, effectiveness, and productivity in accomplishing your objectives and better managing your time.

5.5.3 Overcoming Challenges and Obstacles

Overcoming challenges and obstacles in your financial journey requires resilience, resourcefulness, and strategic planning. Here are some steps to help you navigate financial challenges effectively:

1. Assess the Situation: Take a step back and objectively assess the challenges you're facing. Identify the specific financial obstacles you're encountering, whether it's debt, insufficient savings, income loss, unexpected expenses, or other issues.

2. Seek Knowledge and Education: Educate yourself about personal finance concepts, strategies, and best practices. Understanding how to manage money effectively, budget, save, invest, and deal with debt can empower you to make informed decisions and overcome financial challenges more effectively.

3. Create a Budget: Develop a realistic budget to track your income, expenses, and savings goals. Analyze your spending habits, identify areas where you can cut back or reduce expenses, and allocate funds towards your financial

priorities.

4. Build Emergency Savings: Establish an emergency fund to provide a financial buffer for unexpected expenses or income disruptions. Aim to save three to six months' worth of living expenses in a separate savings account to cover emergencies like medical bills, car repairs, or job loss.

5. Prioritize Debt Repayment: If you have debt, prioritize paying it off strategically. Focus on high-interest debt first, such as credit card balances or payday loans, while making minimum payments on other debts. Consider debt consolidation or negotiation strategies to lower interest rates or monthly payments.

6. Increase Income: Explore opportunities to increase your income through additional sources, such as side hustles, freelance work, part-time jobs, or passive income streams. Generating extra income can help you accelerate debt repayment, boost savings, and improve your financial stability.

7. Seek Professional Guidance: Consider consulting with a financial advisor, counselor, or coach for personalized guidance and advice. A professional can help you develop a tailored financial plan, identify opportunities for improvement, and navigate complex financial situations.

8. Stay Flexible and Adapt: Be prepared to adjust your financial plan and strategies as needed in response to changing circumstances or unexpected events. Stay flexible, resourceful, and open-minded, and be willing to explore alternative solutions to overcome obstacles.

9. Stay Positive and Motivated: Maintain a positive attitude and mindset, even in the face of challenges. Celebrate small victories and progress towards your financial goals, and remind yourself of the bigger picture and the benefits of financial stability and security.

10. Focus on Long-Term Goals: Keep your long-term financial goals in mind as you navigate short-term challenges. Stay focused on your objectives, whether it's buying a home, retiring comfortably, funding education, or achieving financial independence, and use them as motivation to overcome obstacles along the way.

11. Negotiate with Creditors: If you are having trouble obtaining finance, you might want to think about reaching a more reasonable agreement with your creditors or lenders. lower payments, lower loan rates, or payment arrangements as a solution. Many creditors are open to collaborating with you to reach win-win agreements.Reducing Discretionary Spending: Examine your expenses and pinpoint areas where you may cut back on or do away with discretionary spending. Seek out superfluous items or services that you can temporarily forgo in order to free up cash for other pressing needs.

13. Explore Government aid Initiatives: If you are having financial difficulties, look into government aid programs including grants, subsidies, and other initiatives. For short-term requirements like housing, electricity, food, or medical care, these programs can help.

14. Create a support system: When things get tough, seek out friends, family, or local resources for moral support, direction, or practical assistance. Don't be afraid to ask for assistance when you need it, and make sure you repay the favor by lending a helpful hand to others in need.

15. Invest in Yourself: To increase your earning potential and financial flexibility, invest in enhancing your education or credentials. Think about if getting more training, certifications, or opportunities for professional development will help you advance in your career or get a better position.

16. Protect Your Assets: Prevents unanticipated risks and events by actively safeguarding your assets and financial stability. To avoid financial loss, this

can entail getting health, life, disability, property, and liability insurance.

17. Stay Organized: To help you stay organized, keep thorough records of your earnings, outlays, assets, liabilities, and financial objectives. Financial programs, budgeting software, and spreadsheets are helpful resources for keeping track of spending and reaching objectives

18. Practice Delayed Gratification: Learn to postpone your happiness and make wise financial choices. Put long-term financial security ahead of impulsive spending, and concentrate on steadily increasing wealth via prudent investing, regular saving, and astute money management.

19. Remain Updated: Be aware of any modifications to financial regulations or guidelines that might have an impact on your financial status, the market, or overall economic trends. You can make wise decisions and deftly adjust to changing conditions when you possess information.

20. Milestones and Progress: Honor your accomplishments, significant anniversaries, and strides toward addressing financial challenges. Acknowledge your commitment and diligence, and use these successes as motivation to keep working toward your financial objectives.

5.6 Investing for the Future

5.6.1 Stocks

Stocks, also referred to as shares or equities, are ownership stakes in a business. Buying stocks entitles you to a little share of the company's ownership. At the event that the business pays dividends, you could have the ability to vote at shareholder meetings and receive dividends. Stock prices may change depending on a number of variables, including investor attitude, market circumstances, and corporate performance.

1. Risks:

Variability of Market: Short-term market dynamics, economic developments, or investor mood may all cause large swings in stock values. Investment values may fluctuate suddenly and unpredictably as a result of this volatility.

Risks Specific to the Company: The risks associated with investing in a company's stock vary and might include those related to management, competition, regulations, and unforeseen occurrences such as scandals or product recalls.

Risk of Sector Concentration: Investing extensively in a single business exposes investors to industry-specific risks such legislative changes, technological upheavals, and changes in customer preferences.

Quantity Issues: There may be little trading activity in some companies due to their lack of liquidity, which makes it difficult to purchase or sell shares fast without having a big effect on the price.

Variations in Currency: Currency risk is a risk associated with investing in foreign stocks because fluctuations in exchange rates may impact the value of holdings denominated in foreign currencies.

2. Potential Returns:

Appreciation of Capital: Even with the associated dangers, stocks have the ability to increase in value significantly over time, giving investors the chance to increase their wealth as their investments grow.

Dividend Income: A lot of stocks provide dividends, which give investors a consistent source of income. For investors who prioritize steady cash flow and are income-oriented, dividend-paying companies might be very alluring.

Long-Term Development: Historically, over long periods of time, equities have outperformed other asset types like bonds or cash in terms of returns. Putting money into reputable businesses with solid foundations might have the potential to develop over time.

Diversification Advantages:** Spreading your investments over a variety of stocks, industries, and asset classes may help reduce risk and maximize rewards from a range of sources.

Investors hoping to reach their financial objectives via stock investing must comprehend and manage risk and possible return efficiently.

5.6.2 Bonds

Bonds are debt instruments issued by governments, municipalities, and enterprises to raise funds. When you purchase a bond, you are essentially lending money to the issuer for a predetermined period. In exchange, the issuer pledges to pay you monthly interest payments, known as coupon payments, and to repay the principal amount (face value) when the bond matures. Bonds typically have a fixed interest rate and maturity date, giving investors a consistent source of income and a set timeframe for the return of their capital investment.

Types of Bonds

There are a variety of bond types, each with its own set of characteristics and issuers:

1. Government Bonds: These bonds, which are given by public states, are viewed as among the most secure speculations as the public authority has the influence to force burdens and make cash. Examples include the Treasury bonds issued by the United States government and sovereign bonds issued by other nations.

2. Municipal Bonds: These are bonds that are given by state or city

legislatures to pay for foundation projects like utilities, streets, and schools. Tax breaks might be accessible from civil bonds, particularly assuming that you live in the state where the bond is given.

3. Corporate Bonds: Partnerships issue these bonds to produce cash for a scope of purposes, including obligation renegotiating, acquisitions, and development. Government bonds will generally have lower yields than corporate bonds, yet corporate bonds have a bigger credit risk.

4. High-Yield Bonds (Junk Bonds): These bonds, which accompany a more noteworthy default hazard to investors , are given by organizations with more vulnerable credit scores. Subsequently, they give more significant returns.

5. Foreign Bonds: These are bonds given in monetary standards other than the home cash of the investor by foreign firms or states. Notwithstanding credit risk, putting resources into unfamiliar bonds opens investors to money risk.

6. Convertible Bonds: These bonds can be exchanged for a predetermined number of shares of the issuer's common stock at the option of the bondholders. The capital appreciation capability of convertible bonds is dependent upon an expansion in the guarantor's stock cost.

7. Zero-Coupon Bonds: There are no standard interest installments made on these bonds. Instead, they are issued at a discount to face value and redeemed at face value upon maturity, providing investors with a return through capital appreciation.

Each type of bond has its own risk-return profile, and investors should carefully consider their investment objectives and risk tolerance before investing in bonds.

Risks and Returns in Bonds

1. Interest Rate Risk:

Risk: Bonds have a fixed rate, as compared to other financial securities, thus when the market interest rates move up, the value of the bonds fall because for investors there is a new opportunity to buy the new bonds with higher yields. This may result in capital losses when you sell earlier than the maturity time.

Return:The risk of holding long-term ones, in general, is compensated by a higher yield than the one of short-term bonds. This happens because investors ask for more return for setting their money out for the longer term, evolving thus their possible losses due to rising interest rates.

2. Credit Risk:

Risk:This is with reference to the riskiness of the bond issuer of defaulting on its debt obligations. Corporate bonds oR Bonds from the economically weak nations (most often called junk bonds) are at greater risk of default than government bonds.

Return:Higher-yielding bonds are priced with a higher risk in order to attract investors. The investors need to be paid a higher return to cover the high chances of default. However, bonds issued by stable governments or highly-rated corporations offer a smaller yield since they are considered safer investments.

3. Inflation Risk:

Risk:Inflation which reduces the purchasing power of fixed-income investments like bonds destroys them. If inflation grows more than the yield of the bond, the real return becomes negative.

Return: Bond yields typically exceed inflation by an appreciable degree to compensate investors for a real return. Nevertheless, low quality bonds or those with long tenors may provide higher nominal yields to cushion possible losses from inflation.

4. Liquidity Risk:

Risk: There is a lack of liquidity for some bonds because there is not enough market to buy and sell them. This may make it tough to get the bond sold off rapidly without influencing its pricing.

Return: Deeper illiquidity bonds usually bring out the higher yields to repay investors for the inconvenience and risk which come with possibly not being able to sell them at the price desired when the time comes.

5. Call Risk:

Risk: A bond can be callable, which means the issuer can redeem it before its maturity. If the interest rates decline in this case, the issuer can opt for the refinancing of the bond at a lower cost, thus requiring investors to invest at a lowered rate of return.

Return: Bond classes susceptible to call risk, which usually offers more generous yields to reward investors for the likelihood of early liquidation and the reinvestment risk that it entails.

6. Reinvestment Risk:

Risk: Falling interest rates can negatively affect future bond cash flows from coupons or principal repayments that have to be reinvested at the lower rates, thus resulting in lower overall returns.

Return: Bond issues perceived to have higher reinvestment risk of lower returns repayment offer higher initial yields as compensation of potential losses from lower reinvestment rates in the future.

7. Exchange Rate Risk (for foreign bonds):

Risk: Foreign currency bonds bear an exchange risk that may influence the returns. If there is a depreciation of the value of the foreign currency against that of the investor's domestic currency, it can reduce returns.

Return: A higher yield of foreign bonds than domestic bonds is usually offered to compensate investors for the additional risk concerned with the exchange rate variation risk. Though currency fluctuations can magnify or cancel out bond returns, asset managers should analyze the net result on the overall portfolio values.

8. Event Risk:

Risk: The event risk reflects the likelihood of fluctuation in events such as company restructuring, mergers, or changes in regulations which may influence the issuer's performance.

Return: Event risk may be priced into bond yields to cover eventualities; the higher yields are meant to allay investors' uncertainties regarding the trigger, occurrences and their influence on the bond's performance.

9. Duration Risk:

Risk: Duration is a meaningful tool to determine a bond's sensitivity to changes in interest rates. Longer-term bonds are more vulnerable to interest rate shifts and thus highly unstable in price fluctuation.

Return: Bonds with longer terms tend to have higher yields that act as a buffer for the risks associated with fluctuations in prices due to fluctuations in interest rates.

10. Default Risk:

Risk: The default risk is the risk that the issuer fails to make scheduled interest or principal payments on schedule. This type of risk is considerably important in the case of low-rated bonds and for those coming from companies or countries with financial difficulties

Return:Same holds true for bonds with higher default risk which provide higher yields as compensation for the much higher default probability. To secure higher yields, investors are supposed to bear the risk of losses caused by default.

Appreciating these risks and the way they affect returns is a prerequisite for bond investors in making informed decisions and creating portfolios that are compatible with their tolerance to risk and investment goals.

5.2.3 Mutual Funds

Mutual funds are financial instruments where investment funds of multiple investors are pooled together to invest in a basket of different securities, such as stocks, bonds or a combination of both. These funds are managed by individual managers that decide as to what to invest on behalf of the investors.

Investors buy units of the mutual fund, and the value of those units depend on how the underlying portfolio of investments performs. Diversification is provided in mutual funds since they invest in a wide range of assets, thus lowering the risk attached to investments in individual securities

They also offer liquidity, meaning that the investors are free to buy or sell stocks on the business days at the fund's current net asset value (NAV). Investors have a choice of several types of mutual funds, such as equity funds, bond funds, balanced funds, index funds and sector funds, all suited for different objectives and tolerance to risks.

Investors can select mutual funds with respect to elements such as goals of investment, risk tolerance, time horizon and desire to directly control the management process of their investments. Fees such as management fees, operating expenses, and sales charges, are some of the fees that mutual funds may charge, and they can affect the returns. Hence, mutual funds are a commonly chosen investment vehicle for those who wish to invest in professional management and comprehensive exposure to the financial market.

Advantages of Mutual Funds

Mutual funds offer several advantages:

1. Diversification: A mutual fund gathers money from several investors and buys from a wide range of assets that minimizes individual risk.

2. Professional Management: The expert portfolio managers act as "agents" of the investors, thus saving their time and labor.

3. Accessibility: Investors can get different assets as well as investment strategies through mutual funds which are not easily available individually.

4. Liquidity: The majority of mutual funds provide for daily liquidity, when investors can sell or purchase shares for the net asset value at the current time.

5. Affordability: Investors with limited sums can enter the market and enjoy the cost advantages in brokerage and management that come with a size.

6. Transparency: Mutual funds keep the investors informed on their holdings and performance through frequent updates which in turn fosters transparency.

7. Regulation: Mutual funds have been regulated by governmental agencies that operate in the investor protection and oversight

8. Flexibility: Mutual funds provide diversification through multiple investment options such as equity, fixed income, and hybrid funds that satisfy various risk appetites and objectives.

9. Automatic Reinvestment: Several mutual funds have the ability for reinvestment of dividends and capital gains, which can accumulate to earn compound returns over time.

10. Risk Management: Risks are managed through such tactics as asset allocation, diversification, and active management by mutual funds. Through these strategies the investors can minimize the possible losses.

11. Access to Expertise: Mutual funds give an investor entry to an army of expert researchers and analysts. Therefore, investors exploit the skills and knowledge of professional fund managers

12. Tax Efficiency: Funds can be designed as tax efficient, with choices to index funds or tax managed funds that aim to keep the investors taxes minimum.

13. Convenience: Mutual funds have the advantage of convenience as their features include Systematic Investment Plans (SIPs) that enable investors to, by investing a fixed amount regularly, avoid the necessity of continuous monitoring as funds are actively managed by fund managers.

Disadvantages of Mutual Funds
While mutual funds offer numerous benefits, they also come with some disadvantages:

1. Fees and Expenses: For the most part, mutual funds have management, operational, and other costs that are attached to them and can diminish the overall rates of return over time.

2. Lack of Control: Investors give up the autonomy for making individual investment choices to the fund manager that may not match their personal investment missions or style.

3. Overdiversification: Although diversification is a positive, the mutual funds can get over diversified, leading to decreased possible significant profit.

4. Performance Risks: Professional management does not save mutual funds from underperformance, the reasons for which may include market circumstances, as well as errors of managers and commissions.

5. Tax Inefficiency: Mutual fund investors may receive taxable capital gains distributions, even if the shareholders have not sold their positions, thereby opening up for tax liabilities.

6. Limited Transparency: Some funds may lack full disclosure on the compositions of their holdings or investment objectives making it difficult for individuals to fully grasp their investments.

7. Redemption Fees: Funds may impose a fee for redemption if the investor sells the shares within a given time frame, and this can lower returns, especially in the case of short-term investing.

8. Potential for Conflicts of Interest: Fund managers might deal with the conflict of interest in which they might put the interests of their companies instead of investors' ones.

9. Market Risk: Mutual funds are exposed to market fluctuations and volatility which can make the investor face losses during downswings in the market conditions.

10. Limited Control Over Timing: Within mutual funds, investors have a limited say on the timing of buying and selling assets within the fund, thus causing an ability problem to capitalize on market opportunities or manage risk in a timely way.

5.2.4 Exchange Traded Funds

Exchanged Traded Funds (ETFs) are investment products, which offer diversification associated with mutual funds with the flexibility and tradability like stocks. They pool investors' funds to buy a portfolio of assets with diversity such investments in stocks, bonds, or commodities. ETFs are devised to mimic the behavior of a particular index, sector, commodity, or other underlying asset. In contrast to mutual funds, which are traded on a transfer agent at the closing price and the net asset value (NAV), ETFs trade on stock exchanges throughout the day at market prices. It ensures that investors are able to buy and sell the shares every time there is a market hour, consequently providing a liquid and flexible market. ETFs are generally cheaper than standard mutual funds in terms of expense ratios and therefore become popular investment vehicles for many investors.

Features of ETFs

Key features of exchange traded funds (ETFs) include:Your Crown Prince is anxious about the ban on Polio vaccines in our country.

1. Diversification: ETFs usually contain a composite package of securities, offering investors immediate diversification across several assets, industries, or geographical areas.

2. Liquidity: ETFs trade on stock exchanges the same way as individual stocks do, giving the investors the option to buy or sell shares at the market prices and thus support liquidity and flexibility.

3. Transparency: The majority of ETFs reveal their holdings on a daily basis, which makes it possible for investors to precisely define assets that the fund holds and calculate their corresponding weights.

4. Low Costs: ETFs often have lower expense ratios than traditional mutual funds, making them a popular choice for investors that are interested in

cost-efficient investments.

5. Flexibility: Investors can apply ETFs for many investment strategies such as long-term investment, short-term trading, hedging and asset allocation.

6. Tax Efficiency: Because of their specific structure ETFs are tax-efficient compared to mutual funds because they usually feature low capital gain distributions.

7. Access to Markets: Exchange traded funds allow investors access to sectors or markets that they may not be able to access directly such as the commodity, international or sector markets.

8. Dividend Reinvestment: Investors can opt for dividends reinvestment plans (DRIPs), usually provided by many ETFs when they are buying an ETF. Hence, an ETF investor can realize compound growth. Primarily, ETFs represent a good investment choice because they are characterized by diversification, liquidity, transparency and cost efficiency.

9. Intraday Pricing: In contrast to the mutual funds that are priced at the end of the trading day, ETFs can be bought and sold throughout the trading day at market-determined prices and such pricing indicates up to date information to the investors.

Risks and Returns in ETFs

Risks:

1. Market Risk: ETFs are prone to market volatility and the value of the ETFs can depreciate due to changes in the prices of the underlying assets or external factors.

2. Sector Risk: ETFs that are specific sector or industry focused are exposed

to the risks that are associated with those sectors such as, government rules changes, economic declines or novel technological developments which can determine the nature of an industry.

3. Liquidity Risk: Despite the fact that ETFs are generally liquid, some ETFs may have smaller trading volumes resulting in wider bid-ask spreads or it may be difficult to execute a trade at a favorable price as their underlying assets are less liquid.

4. Interest Rate Risk: The ETFs of fixed income are vulnerable to changes in the interest rates. If the rates of interest go up, bond prices usually go down, and consequently the value of bond ETFs falls, as well as the income that the investors earn.

5. Credit Risk: A type of ETFs, which invests in bonds or debt securities, is subject to credit risk that can be defined as the possibility of default by the issuer. While low quality credit bonds may have higher returns compared to other bonds, they may also be accompanied by a higher risk of default.

6. Currency Risk: Non-domestic ETFs are subject to currency risk, since changes in exchange rates may affect the price of the underlying assets in the investor's currency of base.

7. Tracking Error Risk: Aims to follow a specific index, ETFs may diverge from the index by several factors such as price or transaction commissions and portfolio management, which leads to tracking error.

8. Counterparty Risk: Some ETFs are derivatives-based or require security lending in order to meet their investment objectives, and investors run the risk of counterparty failure if the derivative counterparty or borrower defaults on their debts.

Returns:

1. Market Returns: The returns of an ETF are highly correlated with the underlyings. In case the assets in the ETF portfolio grow in value, the ETF's share price usually grows too and this growth results in capital gains to investors.

2. Income Returns: There is a type of ETFs which invests in dividend paying stocks or fixed-income securities that generate income returns, namely as dividends or interest payments. It in turn will impact investors' returns.

3. Diversification Benefits: Exchange-traded funds offer a diversification feature in that they put together a portfolio of assets with the intent of lowering overall portfolio risk and boosting returns in comparison to investing in individual securities.

4. Tax Efficiency: The unique structure of ETFs makes them comparatively more tax-efficient than mutual funds, leading to fewer capital gains distributions and higher net realized returns for investors.

5. Cost Savings: ETFs normally have lower expense ratios in comparison to mutual funds which enables investors to earn a better net return, accounting for the power of compounding during the long term.

6. Dividend Reinvestment: Some ETFs allow Investors to choose dividend reinvestment plans (DRIPs) which automatically reinvest their dividends by purchasing the additional shares that provide high-yield returns through compounding.

7. Access to Markets: ETFs can offer access to a wide variety of markets, sectors and asset classes that an individual investor might not be able to gain direct access to and provide for broader diversity and potential upside.

8. Portfolio Customization: ETFs provide an opportunity for constructing portfolios that are individualized in their alignment with particular invest-

ment targets and risk tolerances, as well as asset allocation inclinations, granting investors the freedom to design portfolios that deliver the desired risk and return profiles.

5.2.5 401(k) Plans

A 401(k) plan is a retirement account sponsored by an organization. It enables the employees to contribute and allocate a certain percentage of their paycheck before the taxes are deducted. In addition, the employers can also contribute to their employees' 401(k) account either through matching some percentage of employee's contributions or through profit-sharing contributions. These plans usually feature a selection of investment alternatives that include mutual funds, stocks, and bonds that are presented for choice and selected by the employee from those provided by the plan. Contributions and earnings grow tax sheltered until withdrawal, usually in retirement, when they are taxed like regular wages.

How 401(k) Plans Work

A 401(k) plan is a retirement savings account, which provided by the sponsorship of an employer.Here's how it typically works:

1. Employee Contributions: Employees may set up a flexible spending plan to save a portion or all of their pre-tax salary, up to the limit specified by the IRS for the respective calendar year. Some employers also have a Roth 401(k) option in which contributions are made from after-tax dollars, which means that money can be withdrawn without paying any taxes in the retirement.

2. Employer Contributions (if offered): Some employers contribute a portion of salaries which are matched by the employees, usually up to some percentage of the employee's salary. Primarily, we speak here of the additional funds given to an employee's pension savings.

3. Investment Options: Under the 401(k) plan, participants have a choice

from a range of investment options which includes mutual funds, target date funds and company stock.

4. Tax Benefits: The employee's money went into a traditional 401(k) with pre-tax dollars and was deducted from the taxable income of the year. It means that comes or put in plus earnings are tax-deferred until the time of the retirement withdrawal. Roth 401(k) contributions are made with after-tax dollars, allowing for tax-free distributions in retirement, including any potential investment returns.

5. Withdrawals: The amount from 401(k) plans that are taken as distribution are taxed as regular income. For withdrawals taken before age fifty-nine and half, they are also subject to a 10% additional early withdrawal penalty (though there are some exceptions). Usually, the RMDs start from age 72 (or 70 1/2 if you were born prior to the year 1950) for the traditional 401(k) accounts.

6. Portability: Employee can roll his 401(k) account sum for most parts into another retirement account including IRA and his new employer's 401(k) without recording taxes or penalty.

7. Vesting: Employer contributions can be subject to a vesting schedule that determines how much of the employer's contribution the employee would get to keep the subject from having left the company before a certain period of time. Employees are forever 100% vested in what they contribute.

8. Contribution Limits: IRS indicates annual contribution limits of 401(k) plans. In 2022, the employee contribution limit for the plan between the ages 0-50 for traditional and Roth 401(k) plans is $20,500. Contributions of extra catch-up from employees who are 50 and above years old are allowed.

9. Loans and Hardship Withdrawals: Many 401(k) programs also offer participants the option of taking loans or making hardship withdrawals in

specified conditions. These actions often involve associated costs such as fees, taxes, and reduced retirement savings.

10. Investment Management Fees: The employees of the 401(k) plan are expected to pay the fees of the investments which are handled in the plan. These fees will differ based on the investment choices available, affecting the return for the account in the long term.

11. Employer Responsibilities: Employers who provide the 401(k) plans have certain responsibilities such as selecting and monitoring investment options, provisioning of information about the plan, and complying with the IRS regulations and reporting requirements.

12. Automatic Enrollment and Escalation: Some businesses provide automatic enrollment in their 401(k) plans which means employees are automatically enrolled, unless they decline. Automatic enrollment programs slowly increase employees' contribution rates as time goes by will help them save more for faster retirement.

Overall, 401(k) plans can be great retirement saving tools with attractive benefits - tax benefits, employer contributions (if offered), and diversified investment choices. Nevertheless, the participants should be familiar with the characteristics and limitations of their particular option and to frequently review and modify their contributions and portfolio compositions.

Employer Matching Contributions

A highly salient characteristic of many 401(k) plans is employer matching contributions. Here's how they typically work:

1. Matching Formula: Employees are assigned a matching formula that governs how much the employer will contribute to the employee's 401(k) account based on the employee's percentage of contribution. As an example, a typical formula is that a dollar-for-dollar match of the first 3% of the

employee's salary will be contributed to the plan, and 50 cents on the dollar for the next 2%.

2. Matching Limits: Employers may impose their discretion on how much contributions to match, for example, one percent of the employee's annual salary or up to $500 annually. When the employee comes to this stage, the employer will cease to match more contributions.

3. Vesting Schedule: Contributions that match may be subject to a vesting schedule, which shows the percentage of the employer's contributions the employee is entitled to before a particular time period. There can be different vesting schedules but in a common structure, employees become fully vested with respect to employer contributions after a certain number of years of employment.

4. impact on Retirement Savings: Contributions from employers can make substantive additions to an employee's retirement savings. They effectively replenish free money that is added to the personnel account from which a holiday nest egg increases.

5. Encouraging Participation: In addition to tax deductible contribution, an employer matching contribution is also a means of incentive for the employees to participate in the 401(k) plan and to contribute the maximum amount the employer will match. This also helps in increasing the employee pension contributions and thus can boost the employee retention and job satisfaction.

6. Matching Contribution Types: Employers may provide the employee with several types of matching contributions, which may include traditional matching, discretionary matching, and safe harbor matching. Traditional matching conforms to a specific rule, while discretionary matching provides the employers with more flexibility as they are able to determine contributions. Safe harbor matching is a set of IRS requirements that contributions

must meet in order to guarantee the plan doesn't benefit highly compensated employees.

7. Tax Treatment: Just like with employee contributions, employer matching contributions generally are also tax-deferred. Thus,they won't be subjected to income tax until withdrawn in retirement. However, employer contributions are taxed the same as any other employer's contributions. Such taxes include FICA (social security and medicare taxes).

8. Negotiation and Variation: The employer matches can change a lot from one company or industry to another. Employers may include generous match contributions as part of a benefits package to attract and retain talent, while others may offer no/minimal match contribution. Before accepting an employment offer, employees should pay attention to the employer's matching contribution policy which is one of the many aspects of the employee's total compensation package.

9. Employee Eligibility: Employers can set eligibility requirements on their staff for contributions matching for example, there should be any waiting period before one becomes eligible or a minimum number of hours worked. The employers may also have different matching policies for part time employees or employees that belong in the certain job categories.

10. Communication and Education: Employees are usually informed by the employers about 401(k) plans, including the information on how the matching contributions are made. It is important for employees to review the information attentively and to avail of any education or guidance provided by the Employer or Plan Administrator.

This makeup in general is the employer's matching contribution is needed for the employees to speed up their savings in retirement, but the employees must understand the individual terms and conditions of the company's matching contribution policy.

5.7 Building an investment Portfolio

5.7.1 Assets Allocation

Building an investment portfolio through asset allocation requires four important steps:

1. Know your tolerance: Determine the level of risk you can tolerate. Consider your finances, time and investment goals.

2. Determine your asset allocation strategy: Select a combination of asset classes based on your investment objectives and risk profile. Bonds, real estate, stocks, and cash equivalents are examples of common asset classes.

3. Consider the Core Satellite Method: To improve diversification or gain a unique opportunity, allocate a portion of your portfolio to core investments, such as broad market index funds or ETFs, and in addition to satellite investments, individual funds, sector funds, etc.

4. Adjust to current market conditions: Be prepared to adjust your asset allocation as market conditions and your financial goals and risk appetite change over time. Regular comparisons can maintain regular distributions.

5. Use Your Way:*m Invest in the distribution method of your choice among various assets. There are many investment vehicles that can help you achieve this, including mutual funds, exchange-traded funds (ETFs), individual stocks and bonds, and managed funds.

6. Checks and Adjustments: Regularly review your portfolio to ensure it is aligned with your asset allocation goals. If necessary, adjust your account to return to the correct distribution.

7. Stay Updated: Stay informed about economic and market trends affecting

your property. Monitor changes in interest rates, asset values and geopolitical events that affect financial performance.

8. Seek Expert Advice: Consider speaking with a financial advisor to find the right asset allocation plan based on your unique situation and goals. They can provide individual advice and guidance according to your needs.

9. Risk and Return: Recognize how risk and return are related. In general, an asset's return increases with its level of risk. The distribution of assets should be carefully considered in relation to the risks and rewards.

10. Benefits of Diversification: You can lessen the effect of volatility on individual assets and the portfolio as a whole by distributing your investments across a number of asset types. Diverse asset classes exhibit distinct market behaviors and return characteristics.

11. Connections: Examine the links among different resources. Correlation measures how much the prices of various assets deviate from one another. Because of the state of the market, choosing assets with low or negative correlation will enhance the benefits of diversification.

12. Update: To make sure your asset allocation stays on course, rebalance your portfolio on a regular basis. Purchasing or selling assets to reallocate your portfolio is the process of redemption. This guarantees that over time, your portfolio will continue to represent your investing goals and risk tolerance.

13. Extended Objectives: Retain a long-term investing mindset and try not to react too strongly to changes in the market. Adhere to your plan for allocating assets. Inaccurate timing in the market might result in expensive errors.

14. Take into account your whole life cycle: Depending on your age, financial

objectives, and anticipated retirement date, your asset allocation may alter over time. For instance, an experienced investor would choose to hold bonds and better-quality choices, whereas a novice investor with a long-term investment perspective might allocate their funds to stocks because of their growth potential.

15. Legal Aspects: When determining how to divide your assets, take the tax implications into account. Because different asset classes are subject to different taxation regimes, it is wise to maintain your tax-advantaged investments in tax-advantaged accounts, like an IRA or 401(k).

16. Monthly Evaluation: Examine your portfolio and asset allocation. You might need to modify your asset allocation as market or financial conditions change in order to meet your investment objectives. You can construct a diverse investing portfolio that matches your patience and long-term financial objectives with the help of an asset allocation plan and thorough research on these factors.

5.7.2 Diversification

The fund structure should be flexible because it helps spread risk across multiple assets and minimizes the impact of failure on individual investments and the portfolio as a whole. The components of the difference and the method are as follows:

1. Risk Diversification: You can reduce the risk associated with a single investment by spreading your money across multiple assets with different risk and return profiles. For example, if one asset class falls, other asset classes will perform better to cover the losses.

2. Investing All asset classes react differently to economic and market conditions, so diversifying your assets can contribute to the success of your portfolio.

3. Individual Signature: Individual values may vary within each asset class. Investing in a small number of stocks or bonds does not reduce the risk of the unique factors associated with a single investment. Instead, it is better to spread your investments over several products.

4. Risk Control: While diversity cannot completely eliminate risk, it can help manage it. If some investments do well but others don't, your overall investment experience will be stronger.6.

5. Opportunity to Increase Returns: Investors can manage risk and increase returns by diversifying their holdings. Diversification of assets under management allows investors to benefit from multiple sources of improved financial performance.

6. Rebalancing: Consistency in your investment portfolio over time ensures consistent diversification. When some assets are better or worse than others, the process of buying and selling assets to return the portfolio to its distribution is called balancing. This will maintain its strength and power.

7. Geographic and Sector Diversification: Within each asset class, diversification can be achieved by investing in different geographic regions and industry sectors. This approach helps reduce exposure to specific risks associated with a particular region or sector.

8. Correlated Resources: Little to no correlation between assets is ideal for differentiation. Correlation measures how much the prices of different assets change in relation to one another. Putting money into low-cost assets will ease your financial burden and help you attain steady outcomes.

9. Return-Risk Modification: Diversification tends to boost adjusted returns by raising the risk to potential reward ratio. Investors want to assess the performance of their portfolio in terms of the quantity of risk they have been exposed to as well as the actual return. Getting strong returns that are

adjusted for risk is one of the key goals of diversification.

10. Diversification: You can alter your portfolio, even if diversification is crucial. Your higher performing investments will have less of an impact and trading costs will rise with a significant investment. It's critical to strike a balance between diversification and focus in order to manage your portfolio and stay committed to your investing objectives.

11. Take into account other assets: In addition to conventional assets like stocks and bonds, you should think about including non-traditional assets in your portfolio to diversify it. In addition to conventional investments, alternative investments such as shares, real estate, hedge funds, private equity, and so on can provide special risk-return characteristics that might boost stock market volatility.

12. A Review and Evaluation of the Period: Over time, shifts in investor preferences and market conditions may have an impact on the efficacy of your diversification plan. The asset allocation in your portfolio should be reviewed on a regular basis and adjusted as needed to take advantage of new investment opportunities, market conditions, and changing circumstances.

13. Behavioral Considerations: Behavioral biases like overconfidence and underconfidence can be controlled via diversity. If investors spread their portfolios across a range of assets, they may be less susceptible to emotional decisions affected by short-term market volatility or the success of an investment.

14. Tailor the difference to your needs. The ideal degree of diversity depends on a number of individual factors, including financial situation, time horizon, risk tolerance, and investment goals. Make sure your diversification plan complements your long-term financial objectives by customizing it to your particular requirements and interests.These extra components will help you optimize returns, control risk, and build a well-balanced investment portfolio

that suits your objectives and financial situation.

5.7.3 Tax Consideration

Effective financial management is necessary for the acquisition and administration of investment money. The following strategies will assist you in making accurate tax payments:

1. Make use of the tax-advantaged account: Benefit from a range of retirement plans, including 401(k)s, IRAs, and Roth IRAs, that provide tax advantages including tax-advantaged growth or tax-free withdrawals. Traditional retirement plan contributions are tax-free, while contributions to Roth accounts are not as they are made with after-tax funds.

2. Assess investment options to lower your tax obligation: If your taxable income is low, invest in low-tax assets like exchange-traded funds (ETFs) and index funds. Compared to actively managed funds, these funds have lower capital deployment and turnover rates. The proceeds from municipal bonds are not subject to federal taxes, depending on the issuer.

3. Tax Loss Harvesting: To optimize your tax losses, purchase investments to counterbalance capital gains in other sections of your portfolio. The Wash Sale Act forbids commission increases if the same bank is sold again in a thirty-day period.

4. Management of Income: You can compute capital gains to lower your tax obligation. Think about the times when you can purchase investments to reduce capital gains or to take advantage of the long-term capital gains tax, which is paid to assets held for more than a year. Rather than placing your money in a tax-deductible fund, think about reinvesting it in mutual funds to maximize your returns. Income taxes will rise as a result.

5. Asset: To optimize after-tax returns, invest in tax-advantaged mutual

funds and tax-advantaged funds in tax-advantaged accounts. For instance, equities are more tax-efficient than bonds or REITs because they have lower long-term capital gains taxes.

6. Tax Information: Keep abreast of any modifications to tax rules and regulations as they can have an impact on your investing decisions. For tax savings and to optimize your tax return, speak with a financial counselor or tax specialist.

7. Consider Charitable Giving: Explore charitable giving strategies such as donating appreciated securities directly to charity, which can provide a tax deduction for the fair market value of the donated assets while avoiding capital gains taxes on the appreciation.

8. Contributions to Qualified Retirement Plans: Try to increase the amount you contribute to employer-sponsored retirement plans, such 401(k)s and other comparable schemes. Your annual tax payment will be lowered by the tax deductible contributions you make to these programs.

9. Conversion to Roth: Think about transferring funds to a Roth IRA from a standard IRA or employer-sponsored retirement plan. Even if you must pay taxes on the amount withdrawn, qualified distributions from a Roth IRA after retirement are tax-free, offering tax diversity and the possibility of long-term tax savings.

10. Tax-Friendly Withdrawal Strategy: Make sure to carefully plan your withdrawals so that you can take out cash from your retirement account at retirement and save taxes on that money. To lower tax responsibility, this may entail combining taxable, deductible, and tax-free accounts. It may also entail carefully modifying deductions to remain inside a given tax bracket.

11. College Savings 529 Plan: You can save money for college by using a 529 college savings plan. Contributions to these programs grow tax-free and tax

deductible when utilized for qualified educational expenses, offering a great chance to save on educational costs.

12. Health Savings Account (HSA): You should think about making contributions to an HSA if the deductible on your health insurance plan is high. Earnings are tax-free, contributions are tax-deductible, and deductions for approved medical costs are tax-free. HSAs offer three tax benefits and can be a helpful tool for covering medical costs associated with retirement.

13. Maintain organization: All financial transactions, including purchases, sales, distributes, and payments, should be meticulously documented. You can report your investment income and deductions on your taxes more promptly and properly if you keep solid records.

14. List of Tax Deductions: When deducting tax accounts, take into account the order in which you dispose of assets to reduce taxes. Prior to purchasing assets with a higher tax impact, start by purchasing assets with a reduced tax impact, such as assets you will hold for a long period with low capital gains rates.

15. Estate Planning: Make the most of your inheritance to your heirs by utilizing the estate planning process to minimize inheritance tax. This can involve using estate tax credits to lower the amount of taxes your family must pay, transferring assets while you are still alive, or creating a trust.

16 Seek guidance from a tax professional: The intricacy of tax rules and regulations varies based on your circumstances. To ensure that your tax plan is customized to your financial condition and objectives, think about collaborating with a tax specialist, such as a CPA or tax counselor. They may offer individualized guidance.By incorporating these extra tax management techniques into your entire financial plan, you may maximize tax-efficient growth, reduce taxes, and eventually raise your after-tax value.

5.7.4 Benefits of Tax Management

Tax management benefits investors and individuals in a number of ways, including:

1. Maximize after-tax income: Investors can protect their investment over time and maximize their after-tax income with diligent management. Your income tax.

2. Minimize tax liability: By utilizing available tax credits, deductions, and credits, prudent tax management can help you minimize your tax payment. By doing this, you may pay less in taxes and have more money available for other financial needs.

3. Cost Reductions: Taxes on investments can be decreased, allowing investors to save more for other necessities or future investments. This makes growth possible more quickly over time, which can assist investors in reaching their long-term financial objectives.

4. Increase cash flow: Tax management strategies can boost cash flow by lowering tax payments, which enables people to save a larger portion of their income for future purchases or savings. This can enhance daily money management's stability and flexibility.

5. Risk Management: A number of tax management techniques can be used to lessen the impact of taxes on the performance of a portfolio as a whole and to limit investment risk. Diversification among several tax-advantaged accounts or asset classes is one example of these tactics. It can improve the consistency of your investing habit and streamline your investing process.

6. Demonstrating Tax Effectiveness: Investing tax efficiently entails setting up assets to minimize taxes on capital gains, investment income, and profit distribution. By making tax-efficient investments, distributing their assets

wisely, and employing tax strategies, investors can maximize after-tax returns and overall tax efficiency.

7. Achieving Financial Goals: Good tax management assists investors in reaching their larger financial objectives by maximizing their financial resources, lowering needless tax burdens, and raising the possibility that they will attain the desired outcomes, whether they be wealth accumulation, retirement savings, or funding for education.

8. Remain knowledgeable: People may guarantee they fulfill their tax commitments and also prevent penalties or legal issues for false reporting or tax evasion by staying informed about tax laws, rules, and reporting requirements. This encourages fiscal responsibility and mental tranquility. In general, attaining long-term financial success, safeguarding your assets, and improving financial efficiency all depend on effective tax management. People can reduce their taxes, raise their after-tax income, and enhance their financial health by incorporating tax efficiency measures into their financial and investment planning.

9. Maximize after-tax income: Investors can both protect and grow their after-tax income over time with prudent management.

10. Reduce your tax liability: By utilizing all applicable tax credits, deductions, and credits, you can minimize your tax liability through prudent tax management. This can lower your tax liability and free up additional funds for other financial needs.

11. Cash Reserves: By lowering taxes on investments, investors can save more money for other needs or future investments. Over time, this enables faster growth, which can assist investors in reaching their long-term financial objectives.

12. Achieve better cash flow: By lowering tax payments, tax management

strategies let consumers save more of their income for savings or immediate needs. This can help daily money management become more stable and flexible.

13. Risk Management: A variety of tax planning techniques can lessen the effect of taxes on the performance of a portfolio as a whole and help to limit investment risk. Diversification among several asset classes or tax-advantaged accounts is one example of these tactics. It may strengthen your investment routine and improve the efficiency of your investing process.

14. Reaching tax effectiveness: Investing tax efficiently entails allocating assets to minimize taxes on capital gains, profit distribution, and investment income. By making wise asset allocation decisions, employing tax strategies, and selecting tax-efficient investments, investors can maximize after-tax profits and total tax efficiency.

15. Achieving Financial Goals: Efficient tax management helps investors achieve their larger financial objectives by maximizing their financial resources, lowering needless tax burdens, and raising the possibility that they will attain the desired outcomes, whether developing wealth or saving for retirement or college expenses.

16. Remain educated: People may make sure they fulfill their tax commitments and stay out of trouble with the law by staying informed about tax laws, rules, and reporting requirements. They can also avoid penalties or legal issues for false reporting or tax evasion. This encourages financial stability and accountability. All things considered, maximizing financial efficiency, safeguarding your assets, and reaching long-term financial success depend heavily on effective tax management. Tax efficiency measures can help people save money on taxes, boost their after-tax income, and strengthen their financial position when incorporated into their financial and investment planning.

6

Chapter 6

Setting Up Your Own Business

6.1 How to Generate Business Ideas

1. Identification of problems or needs: Use surveys, interviews or daily observations to identify people's problems and difficulties. Research issues such as inefficient transportation, difficulty finding reliable child care, or limited access to affordable health care.

2. Discover your passion and skills: Think about how you can benefit from the things you love to do or are good at in your job. For example, if you have a keen interest in photography, you might consider running workshops, selling photos online, or doing photo editing.

3. Follow trends and innovations: Monitor opportunities by focusing on evolving technologies, social changes and changing customer behavior. For example, as remote work becomes more popular, there is a growing demand for products and services that support online teamwork, mental health and the convenience of the home office.

4. Identify Market Gaps: Research the market and industry to find underserved customers or areas that could benefit from development. For example: looking for ideas that can fill the gaps and address deficiencies or unmet needs in health, education or transport.

5. Operating Technology: Discover how cutting-edge technologies such as augmented reality, blockchain and artificial intelligence can be used to develop creative solutions. For example, consider using blockchain technology to create a decentralized exchange for digital goods or rare collectibles.

6. Consider demographic changes: To forecast future market demand, look at demographic changes such as population aging, urbanization or cultural diversity. This is exemplified by the growing popularity of plant-based diets among younger generations, which has created a market for launching plant-based meal delivery services aimed at health-conscious customers.

7. Adaptation of an existing concept: Reimagining an existing idea, product or business structure for a new market or application. For example: using vertical farming technology to transform traditional farming methods to increase crop productivity in urban areas and reduce agriculture's impact on the environment.

8. Collaborate and network: Talk to other entrepreneurs, industry professionals and potential clients to generate ideas, test hypotheses and gain insights. For example, consider partnering with nearby businesses, civic associations or educational institutions to develop creative responses to regional social or environmental issues.

9. Resolving personal problems: Think about the personal disappointments and experiences you've had. Chances are others are facing the same problem as you. Take care and maybe turn it into a business. For example, if you have trouble staying organized, consider creating a physical planner with special

features tailored to your needs or productivity software.

10. Combine ideas from different fields: Look for inspiration in unrelated fields and try to apply ideas, strategies or technological developments in your own field. For example: developing a work space at home for parents, integrating aspects of the nursery and the coworking space.

11. Think Environmental Sustainability: As environmental issues become a growing concern, consider companies that support sustainability, reduce waste, or reduce carbon emissions. For example, opening zero-waste stores that offer products without packaging and ecological alternatives for daily use.

12. Niche development: Focus on underutilized or specialized market niches in more established companies. These markets are likely to experience less competition and higher levels of loyal customer bases. For example: launching a subscription box service that offers breed-specific or hobby-exclusive toys, treats and accessories to meet the needs of pet owners.

13. Design for convenience or time-saving solutions: Identify tasks or procedures that require time or are inconvenient for the individual and then look for solutions to automate or simplify them. Example: Create a smartphone app that connects consumers with a personal assistant near them to clean, shop and run errands.

14. Create sessions or transformations: Think of companies that offer their customers memorable moments, opportunities for personal development or transformation sessions. For example: Create a wellness center that offers intensive classes in self-awareness, holistic healing, and mindfulness.

15. Embrace the sharing economy: Find ways to enable peer-to-peer transactions using available resources or using collaborative consumption models. For example, creating a platform that connects tourists and locals to

offer guided tours, B&B and other unique cultural experiences.

16. Target Demographics or Emerging Markets: Look for growing demographics or new markets with specific requirements or preferences. For example, creating educational apps or online courses specifically for homeschooling families looking for personalized and flexible learning opportunities.

17. Traditional Industry Innovation: The study of how revolutionary business concepts, distribution methods or technologies can modernize or improve existing industries. For example: creating a digital marketplace that connects manufacturers with the global consumer base and eliminates the need for middlemen.

18. Gamify Daily Activities: Add game elements, rewards or difficulty level to make daily tasks more interesting and fun for users. Example: Create a fitness app that allows users to compete with peers, earn virtual rewards, and achieve achievements while making exercise feel like a game.

19. Unleash the power of community:
   Create a forum or meeting place where people with similar interests can interact, work together and share knowledge or resources. - For example: create an online forum where enthusiasts and hobbyists can share tips, guides and ideas for their activities.

20. Revival of heritage or traditional crafts: Recovery of lost arts or modernization of traditional crafts to preserve cultural heritage and crafts. For example, starting a business selling handmade products made by specialized artisans from indigenous communities around the world.

21. Addressing mental health and well-being: Creation of goods and services that promote emotional stability, stress reduction and mental health. For example, Create a smartphone app that provides mood tracking, mindfulness

training, and guided meditation sessions to help users increase mental strength and emotional balance.

22. Powerful Digital Nomadism and Remote Employment: Support the growing trend of remote employment by providing services, technology or resources that encourage location-independent living. For example, developing a portal that connects digital nomads with coexistence spaces, joint work spaces and online meetings around the world.

23. Establish links between generations: Encourage partnerships and exchanges between different age groups to promote understanding, friendship and mutual learning. For example, launch a service that pairs seniors with tech-savvy mentors to help them navigate the Internet, learn new skills, and maintain relationships with loved ones.

24. Promotion of cultural exchange and diversity: Celebrate cultural diversity and promote intercultural understanding through events, products or projects. For example, you can plan cultural festivals, workshops and gatherings that showcase the customs, food, music and arts of different towns and communities.

25. Exploring the future of transport: Harnessing innovation to offer convenient, cost-effective and sustainable mobility solutions. For example, consider designing self-driving electric cars for urban delivery services to reduce last-mile delivery costs, carbon emissions and traffic congestion.

26. Support the needs of older populations: Develop goods and services that meet the unique needs and preferences of older populations, such as social inclusion, mobility and health care. For example, to improve the safety and freedom of elderly people living alone, smart home devices equipped with fall detection sensors, voice assistants and remote control functions have been developed.

27. Promoting financial inclusion and literacy: Provide affordable financial services, information and tools to empower marginalized groups and individuals. For example, you could develop a mobile banking application targeting the unbanked and unbanked, offering low-cost transactions, microfinance and multilingual financial literacy courses. These strategies can inspire creative business concepts that satisfy a wide range of needs, interests and demographics. You can discover unique business and social impact opportunities by thinking creatively and looking for alternative paths.

By digging deeper into each stage, you can find specific job opportunities that match your passions, skills, target markets, and needs. Before starting your business, remember to validate your idea through thorough research, experiments, and feedback from potential customers.

6.2 Market Research

Extensive market research is used to examine the requirements, preferences, and purchasing patterns of the target market. Here is a step-by-step guide:

1. Determine Your Goals: Define your market research goals in advance. Define your goals and the specific facts you need to collect. Setting specific goals will guide your research efforts, whether the purpose is to understand customer preferences, evaluate competitors, or determine market size.

2. Determine who your ideal customer is: Identify the psychographics (lifestyle, values, interests), behaviors (buying patterns, preferences) and demographics (age, gender, income) of your target audience. This can help you tailor your research and inquiry techniques to successfully communicate and engage with your target audience.

3. Choose your research method: Make sure your research techniques are compatible with your goals and target audience. Common techniques include focus groups, surveys, interviews, and observations. Choose between

138

primary research, which involves gathering new data, and secondary research, which involves examining existing reports and data.

4. Create your own research instrument: - Create a research instrument, including discussion guides, interview transcripts and surveys. Make sure the questions you ask are objective, understandable and relevant to your goals. Before starting your investigation, test the tool to identify any issues.

5. Data Collection: Put your research strategy into practice and start collecting information from your target audience. This may include door-to-door interviews, interviews or observing customer behavior. Record comments, feedback and any relevant information.

6. Data Analysis: Organize and examine collected information to uncover trends, patterns and insights. Use qualitative methods, statistical analysis, or data visualization software to interpret the results. Look for outliers, key facts, and connections that can help you make decisions.

7. Interpreting Results: Consider your goals and your company's goals when interpreting data analysis results. How do the results affect your marketing strategy, goods or services? Look for actionable information that can form the basis for strategic goals and informed decisions.

8. Competition Assessment: Understand the strengths, weaknesses and market position of competitors in your field. Research their products, costs, distribution methods, and advertising strategies. Identify where you can make a difference and where you have a competitive advantage.

9. Assessment of market size and potential: Determining the size of the target market and its growth potential. Consider variables such as market trends, the competitive landscape, demographics and the regulatory environment. This helps you understand the attractiveness and feasibility of the market opportunity.

10. Validation of results: Get input from experts, business leaders or potential customers to validate your research results. To ensure the accuracy and relevance of your findings, you must consider their views and feedback.

11. Make informed decisions: Use market research information to make decisions about your business strategy, product development, marketing campaigns and resource allocation. To increase your chances of success, make sure your campaign matches the requirements and preferences of your target market.

12. Iteration and Update: Market research is an iterative process and must be continuously monitored and updated. Pay close attention to changes in the competitive environment, market dynamics and customer behavior. Update your research regularly to stay informed and agile in the ever-changing business environment.

13. Use online resources and tools: Use online resources and platforms to conduct data analysis, surveys and market research. Research resources can be found at sites like Google Trends, SurveyMonkey, and SEMrush, which provide relevant data and statistics.

14. Monitor Online Communities and Social Media: Understand the discussions taking place in online groups, forums and social media platforms about your target market or business. Research customer feedback, trends and attitudes to identify new opportunities and potential problems.

15. Conduct a competitive analysis: Research your competitors' strengths, weaknesses, strategies and market positioning. Look for opportunities to develop untapped market areas or unmet customer needs, as well as gaps in their products and capabilities.

16. New Technology Research: Stay on top of new developments and technologies that have the potential to advance your industry or open up new

business opportunities. Consider the potential impact that new technologies such as virtual reality, blockchain and artificial intelligence can have on consumer behavior and market dynamics.

17. Seek Professional Advice and Information: Talk to mentors, consultants, industry experts and people with specific training and experience in your field. Their perspectives and insights can provide useful guidance and support the validity of your findings.

18. Conduct observational and field studies: Become an expert in your field by carefully analyzing consumer behavior, buying trends, and market dynamics. To learn more about your target market, conduct a mystery shopping campaign, fieldwork, or ethnographic research

19. Test Prototypes: Develop a prototype or mock-up to validate assumptions, test market demand, and get feedback before committing significant resources to production or full release. Review multiple iterations using methods such as A/B testing and make adjustments based on the results.

20. Discover International Markets and Trends: Explore insights into emerging economies and global markets by looking beyond local or regional markets. To adapt your offers and strategies, you need to take into account market developments, legal restrictions and cultural differences.

21. Host a Customer Advisory Board: Bring together a customer advisory group or board of key stakeholders, early adopters and loyal customers. Use their opinions, ideas and suggestions to improve your products, services and marketing strategies.

22. Analysis of Government and Industry Reports: To better understand market trends, regulatory changes and macroeconomic issues that may affect your business, you can access government publications, industry reports, market studies and financial data.

23. Monitoring customer patterns and behavior: Use consumer analytics platforms, trend forecasting organizations, and market research firms to monitor customer trends, preferences, and behaviors. Stay informed about changes in consumer opinions, habits and lifestyles.

24. Participate in Content Marketing and Thought Leadership: Develop thought leadership in your field by producing insightful content, sharing your ideas, and attending conferences, webinars, and events. Engage with your audience to build trust and gain insightful market data.

25. Associations with associations and strategic alliances: Establish alliances, associations or collaboration projects with like-minded companies, groups or influencers. Leverage their relationships, strengths and knowledge to broaden your horizons and gain a different view of the market.

By adding these additional techniques to your market research methodology, you can improve your understanding of your target market, uncover new opportunities, and make better decisions to grow your business.

6.3. Create a Business Plan

Create a thorough business plan that outlines your objectives, target market, operational schedule, marketing strategy, and financial forecasts. A strong business plan gives your company direction and aids in obtaining funding from lenders or investors.

To describe your company, its objectives, guiding principles, and procedures, you need a business plan. This is a comprehensive guide to assist you in creating the ideal business plan.

1. Summary: Offers an executive synopsis including goals, advantages over competitors, markets, and money. projections for your company. Your material needs to be visually appealing and simple to read in order to grab readers' attention.

2. Company Overview: Gives a quick rundown of the company's aims, objectives, and organizational structure (corporation, partnership, sole proprietorship, etc.). Describe the distinctive features of your business and how it meets a particular market demand.

3. Market Research: Learn as much as you can about the target market, customers, industry, and rivals in the market. investigating market trends, opportunities for growth, and obstacles. Recognize the needs, desires, and purchasing habits of your intended market.

4. Organization and Management:
   Provides an overview of the organization and its management structure, outlining important persons, management teams, roles, and duties. Determine the credentials, backgrounds, and strong points of your management group, advisors, and board of directors.

5. Product or Service Line: Give a brief description of the product, taking into account its features, advantages, cost, and USP (unique selling point). Describe how your offering stands out from the competitors and satisfies the needs of your target market.

6. Sales and Marketing Plan: Describe how you plan to draw in clients, create leads, and boost sales. Specify target markets, segments, brands, distribution routes, and positions. This covers techniques for pricing, marketing, sales, and promotions.

7. Financial requirements: If you are seeking funding, describe your idea, investors' expectations, and performance in addition to your financial needs (KING). Incorporate position analysis, financial estimates, and cash flow projections to make the budget more appealing.

8. Financial Planning: Prepare a balance sheet, cash flow projection, and profit and loss statements as part of your business's financial strategy. Project

outcomes, including expenses and benefits, for the following three to five years. Numerous factors need to be taken into account, including revenue growth, operating costs, and price trends.

9. Appendix: Include a supplementary paper or supporting material that offers more details about your company. Senior team member resumes, market research reports, court documents, samples of goods and services, etc. are a few instances.

10. *Review and edit: Check that your business plan is accurate, coherent, and simple to understand. Consult a specialist, advisor, or business consultant for guidance, and make any necessary adjustments to your plan. Your business plan has to be updated on a regular basis as your company expands and the market shifts.

11. Implementation Plan: To accomplish this, make an action plan that details the precise procedures, due dates, and schedules. Determining performance, allocating duties, and establishing performance goals can help to ensure successful implementation.

12. Monitoring and Evaluation: Create a framework and policy to keep an eye on the business and how its operations are doing in comparison to its goals. Monitor your key performance indicators (KPIs), analyze your data, and make the required adjustments to ensure that you stay on course and succeed. You can draw in lenders and investors, clarify your company objectives, and create a plan to launch and grow your enterprise by following these steps and producing a strong business plan.

6.4 Legal form

When establishing a firm, "legal forms" refer to the different companies or structures that might be used, each with unique tax and legal ramifications. A corporation, limited liability company (LLC), partnership, and sole proprietorship are examples of common legal formations. The best legal structure will depend on a number of elements, including regulatory needs, tax treatment, management structure, and liability protection. It's crucial to speak with a lawyer or other legal expert to choose the best legal structure for your company.

1Of course, there are other considerations for each legal form as well:

Sole Proprietorship is a straightforward and reasonably priced business form. - **Control**: The proprietor has total control over the business. - **Tax**: The profits of the business determine how much of the owner's personal income is taxed. - **Liability**: Owners' personal assets may be utilized to satisfy commitments and debts incurred by the company due to their unrestricted personal liability.

2. **Association**: - **Common liability**: partners split management responsibilities and earnings and losses. - **Taxes**: Because associations are pass-through entities for tax purposes, their earnings are handled similarly to those of individual members. Personal revenue in the same manner as a one-person business. **Responsibilities**: The partners split the company's debts and earnings. General partners in a limited partnership are personally liable indefinitely, whereas limited partners are not.

3. **Corporation**: - **Limited Liability**: This indicates that the shareholders' private assets are often shielded from the obligations of the business. - **Separate legal entity**: The business was established after the passing of each of its individual stockholders and is run separately from them. **Taxes**: When a business pays dividends to shareholders, it pays taxes on its profits twice: once at the corporate level and once at the shareholder level. - **Regulatory Compliance**: Among the stricter regulatory requirements that businesses must adhere to include annual meetings, record keeping, and corporate procedure compliance.

In the case of a **Limited Liability Company (LLC)**, partners are afforded limitless liability protection, akin to that of corporate stockholders. - **Tax

145

flexibility**: SARL may elect to file taxes under the corporate, partnership, or sole proprietorship forms (transfer tax). - **Freedom**: A limited liability company affords more flexibility regarding ownership and management structure than a corporation does. **Less procedures**: Compared to a business, there are typically less guidelines and regulations to adhere to.

In the end, a number of factors, such as your long-term objectives, management options, tax concerns, and risk tolerance, will determine the best legal form for your company. Making an educated choice might be aided by consulting with legal and financial professionals.

5. Register Your Business: Make sure your company is properly registered with the relevant government agency and that you have all the licenses and permits required to function in your area. Following the law guarantees that your company operates efficiently and stays out of trouble with the law.

6. Finance: Make a budget to cover your starting and business expenses. Examine the financial sources that are accessible to you, such as crowdsourcing, grants, loans, investors, and your own money. To keep your personal and professional finances apart, open a business bank account

7. Infrastructure and Website: Determine if you need a real website or if your firm can run completely online. Make sure you have the appropriate office space, interior design, and IT infrastructure to support your activities.

8. Brand Development: Craft a distinctive brand identity that appeals to your intended audience. This entails designing a striking logo, a stunning website, and captivating marketing collateral to convey the objectives and offerings of the business.

9. Sales and Marketing: Create a marketing strategy to interact with your target market and draw in new clients. You must use a variety of venues, including social media, email marketing, content marketing, and advertising, to market your company. To turn prospects into happy customers, employ sales techniques.

10. Hiring and Training Teams: Employ qualified employees or contractors to assist you in managing your company if you require additional assistance. A harmonious team can be established through clearly defining roles, encouraging a positive work atmosphere, and offering chances for growth.

11. Management and Operations: Create efficient working methods to ensure consistent supply of products or services. Create the necessary processes to handle the company's finances, inventories, customer relations, and other critical areas.

12. Launch: Plan is an effective launch for your business by creating a buzz through rallies, promotions, and advertising campaigns. makes certain that all policies and frameworks are in place for handling requests and orders from customers.

13. Constant improvement: Determining the areas of work and conducting recurring performance reviews and assessments of the business. You can modify your strategy to suit shifting market demands and maintain your competitiveness by using customer reviews. Obtain their opinions.

14. Compliance and Regulations: Keep yourself updated on the legal requirements that are specific to your field and area. Make sure you abide by labor rules, tax laws, data protection laws, and other legal duties to prevent

fines and legal issues.

15. Network and build: Establish links with other stakeholders, including suppliers, customers, and colleagues in the sector, to broaden your network and build your firm. should use online resources, join professional associations, go to networking events, and network with others in your sector.

By taking these actions and achieving your objectives, you can launch and expand your company. Keep in mind that starting your own business is a journey filled with chances and challenges, so be strong, resilient, and goal-focused.

7

Chapter 7

Mindset Shift for Financial Success

7.1 Importance of Mind-set in Financial Success

The following salient points underscore the significance of mindset in achieving financial success:

1. Concept of Scarcity and Plenty: The abundant mindset holds that there is always enough for everyone and that opportunities are there everywhere. On the other hand, a scarcity mindset emphasizes constraints and worries about scarcity, which results in hoarding, an unwillingness to invest, and lost chances.

2. Embracing sustainability and risk: Having a growth mindset promotes taking calculated risks and viewing setbacks as teaching moments. Resilient people are able to bounce back from financial losses and keep working toward their objectives.

3. Future reward: Over time, delayed satisfaction outweighs instant gratification. Giving up something now for long-term financial gain means

avoiding this kind of reckless expenditure in favor of investing and saving money down the road.

4. Ongoing Education: A growth mentality places a high importance on education and actively searches for knowledge on wealth-building strategies, investment, and personal finance. Never-ending learners are better able to handle their money and adjust to shifting market conditions.

5. Setting and Maintaining Goals: Achieving success in the financial sector necessitates establishing clear financial objectives and a dedication to reaching them. By being tenacious and driven, positive people are better equipped to establish challenging but attainable goals and keep their motivation in the face of difficulty.

6. Awareness and finance: Financial success requires effective management of one's spending, debt, and budget. Careful money management promotes responsible financial behavior and guarantees the efficient use of resources.

7. Confidence and Self-Efficacy: Positivity encourages confidence in oneself and one's capacity to reach financial objectives. People who have this self-efficacy are more inclined to take the initiative, make choices, and go after chances that will help them succeed financially.

8. Flexibility and Adaptability: A growth mindset places a strong emphasis on flexibility and adaptability to changing conditions. In the context of finance, this entails being adaptable and resilient when managing economic shifts and keeping an open mind about new ways to invest.

9. Concept Concerning Wealth: One's financial decisions and habits can be significantly influenced by their perception of wealth. Riches is neither an aim in itself or a source of status recognition; rather, a healthy mentality regards riches as a tool for creating opportunities, supporting personal goals, and making a beneficial effect.

10. Collaboration and Community: Networking and cooperation are crucial for achieving financial success. A collaborative mentality looks for ways to advance mutual gain, share knowledge, and make the most of group resources. It also builds a strong community that may promote both individual and group prosperity.

11. Appreciation and Charity: By encouraging a sense of richness and contentment, having an attitude of thankfulness and generosity can have a good effect on one's financial success. Giving back to the community through volunteer work, financial contributions to charities, or connections with other like-minded individuals improves not only the lives of others but also the giver's own sense of fulfillment and purpose.

12. The Intelligence of Emotions: When it comes to managing wealth and making financial decisions, emotional intelligence is crucial. People who prioritize emotional intelligence, risk management, and empathy are better able to overcome financial obstacles, control risk, and cultivate positive connections with money and other members of their financial ecosystem.

In general, a person's perspective on, approach to, and management of their finances are influenced by their mindset, which in turn influences their capacity to amass wealth and become financially independent. By cultivating a mindset that supports financial success, you can have a significant impact on both your current and future financial circumstances.

7.2 Practicing Financial disciple

You must adhere to financial principles if you want to succeed financially in the long run. The following are some crucial tactics to support you in acquiring and preserving financial literacy:

1. Create a Budget: To begin, include your goals for savings, expenses, and income in a budget. Make prudent financial decisions and set aside the

required funds and invoices for impulsive purchases.

2. Spending Tracking: Keep tabs on your expenditures to ensure that you don't over budget. Track your spending patterns and identify areas for savings by using an app or spreadsheet.

3. Set Clear Goals: Establish measurable, precise financial objectives that are consistent with your principles and aspirations. Whether your objective is to pay off debt, save for retirement, or purchase a home, setting and completing specific goals can help you stay motivated and focused.

4. Automated Savings and Investments: Establish automated transfers to your savings and investment accounts to make sure you are consistently investing and saving a percentage of your income without depending only on willpower.

5. Use delayed gratification: Refrain from impulsive buying and hold off on making needless purchases in order to practice delayed gratification. Think about whether you truly need or want the item, as well as whether it will fit into your budget.

6. Steer clear of debt: Cut back on debt, particularly high-interest consumer debt like credit card debt. Debt should be paid off as soon as feasible, and additional debt should be avoided unless it is strategically required, such as to pay housing or education.

7. Create an emergency reserve: Having an emergency fund gives you financial security and peace of mind in the event of an unforeseen medical emergency or job loss. Save enough money to cover three to six months' worth of living expenses.

8. Live Frugal: Look for methods to save expenses and make ends meet. Reduce expenses, look for discounts, and assess the extra value if you want

to get more for your money.

9. Request Financial Education: Acquire knowledge about investment and personal finance to make wise financial choices. Become more knowledgeable about finances through books, seminars, internet resources, and courses.

10. Be Accountable: Talk to a trusted friend, relative, or financial expert about your financial objectives. They may support and encourage you as you go forward in addition to holding you accountable. You may save money, achieve your financial objectives, and provide security for your family by sticking with these techniques and furthering your financial education over time.

11. Continuous Review and Proofreading: Review the following to ensure patterns are consistent in spending, financial goals, and budget with your priorities and current situation all the time. Make the necessary adjustments to keep up with changes in your income or expenses.

12. Prepare for major expenses: Prepare immediately financially to pay for major expenses such as travel, housing, or large sales. This will reduce the risk of using credit or suddenly losing your savings.

13. Limit Wealth Strategy Skill: Focus on the need to increase your spending to maintain your income. To accelerate progress toward your financial goals, put the extra money into investments, paying down debt, or saving.

14. Spend money: Before making a purchase, consider whether it aligns with your priorities and values. Think about whether the money could be better spent elsewhere or if it would improve your life.

15. Create Multiple Streams of Income: Stocks To increase your primary income, explore opportunities from side hustles, gifts, rentals, or passive investments.

16. Keep learning even if you succeed. Find out when you receive an unexpected gift, whether it's a loan, a tax refund or an inheritance. Instead of spending too much on unnecessary things, consider putting some of your energy into investing and saving.

17. Practice Patience with Investments: Avoid chasing hot investment trends or trying to time the market. Instead, focus on a diversified, long-term investment strategy aligned with your risk tolerance and financial goals.

18. Highlight Milestones: Celebrate and celebrate your financial achievements, no matter how small. Knowing your achievements, such as hitting savings goals, paying off debt, sticking to a monthly spending plan, can support the development of appropriate financial habits.

19. Stay motivated. Reminding yourself of the rationale behind your financial goals and the benefits of staying financially educated will help you stay motivated. When finding your ideal financial position, make sure you take the necessary steps to achieve it. By incorporating these additional ideas into your daily financial training, you can improve your financial situation, accumulate cash, and achieve your long-term financial goals.

7.3 Overcoming Limiting Beliefs

Creating a positive financial mindset requires identifying negative thoughts, questioning them, and replacing them with powerful thoughts. This process is called demystification. For further explanation see:

1. Become aware of your subconscious beliefs: think about your thoughts and feelings about money. Beliefs like "I don't know how to invest." or "I can't save much." These are examples. Writing will help you understand better.

2. Question Their Validity: Once you've identified your limiting beliefs,

challenge them. Ask yourself why you believe them and whether they are based on evidence or assumptions. Often, you'll find that these beliefs are not grounded in reality but are shaped by past experiences or societal influences.

3. Replace with Positive Affirmations: After challenging your limiting beliefs, replace them with positive affirmations that reflect the mindset you want to cultivate. For example, if you believe "I'll never get out of debt," replace it with "I am capable of managing my finances and becoming debt-free."

4. Educate Yourself: When it comes to personal finance, information is power. Spend time learning about investing, finance, financial literacy and other related topics. As you become more knowledgeable about money management, your confidence will increase when making financial decisions.

5. Show your success: An effective way to change your thinking is visualization. Take time each day to visualize yourself achieving your financial goals. Think about what you will do and how you will feel when you achieve those goals. This can motivate you to take action by reinforcing your positive thoughts.

6. Become a positive energy: Gather people who care about money and achievement. Their habits and thoughts can influence you and give you motivation and encouragement as you try to overcome your inferiority complex.

7. Practice: Removing superstitions requires action. Make simple but effective changes to your financial processes and startup options. Honor your achievements, no matter how small, and learn from mistakes along the way.

8. Ask for help: Don't be afraid to ask for help when you need it. Consider working with a coach or financial advisor who can provide guidance and accountability. Participating in events and support groups focused on

financial empowerment can provide guidance and motivation. By constantly questioning and replacing limiting thoughts with positive thoughts and actions, you can create a powerful financial mindset that will help you achieve your goals and create a financial life for the future.

9. Recognize Your Limiting Beliefs: Spend some time thinking about yourself. What limiting attitudes or thoughts do you have around money? These may be values that you carry over from your childhood, from cultural influences, or from previous financial encounters. Get clarity by putting them in writing.

10. Contest Their Veracity: Examine your limiting ideas carefully when you've recognized them. Consider the following inquiries:

- From whom did this belief originate?
- What proof do I have for it, please?
- Has this belief ever caused me to fall behind?
- Are there opposing viewpoints or counterexamples that I haven't thought of?

11. Substitute with affirmations that are positive: After you've questioned the truth of your limiting beliefs, swap them out for affirmations that give you more confidence. Positive, in-the-moment remarks that refute your limiting ideas should be used as affirmations. As an illustration:

- Rather than "I'm bad with money," state "I am capable of managing my finances effectively."
- Rather than "I'll never be wealthy," state "I have the ability to create wealth and abundance in my life."

12. Educate Yourself: Changing your perspective and gaining confidence require knowledge. Make use of resources on issues like investing, saving,

budgeting, and wealth development, such as books, podcasts, online courses, and workshops. Your confidence in your ability to manage your finances wisely will increase as you gain more knowledge about personal finance.

13. Show Off Your Success: One effective method for changing your subconscious mind is visualization. Spend some time every day seeing yourself reaching your financial objectives. Imagine the precise steps you'll take, the obstacles you'll get beyond, and the accomplishments and satisfaction you'll feel along the journey. Visualization can inspire you to take action toward your goals and support your positive views.

14. Adorn Yourself with Positive Energies: Assemble a circle of people who are upbeat about money and achievement. These could be mentors, friends, family, or coworkers who encourage and support you. Avoid negative influences that could support limiting views and participate in discussions and activities that support your values and financial goals.

15. Take Action: Taking initiative is necessary to break free from restricting ideas. Take constant action to reach your goals by breaking them down into small, doable stages. No matter how tiny your accomplishments may seem, acknowledge them along the road and take lessons from whatever obstacles you face. Developing self-assurance and strengthening optimistic views about your capacity for financial success require action.

16. Seek Assistance: Never be afraid to ask for help when you need it to get over limiting thoughts and develop a sound financial mindset. This could be joining a community or support group of like-minded people who can offer encouragement, counsel, and perspective, or working with a financial advisor or coach who can offer tailored assistance and accountability.

Through adherence to these guidelines and a dedication to surmounting limiting ideas, you can progressively reframe your perspective to one of prosperity, self-assurance, and monetary authority. It takes time and work to change your thinking, but the benefits of reaching your financial objectives and building a secure future are priceless.

Final thoughts on Breaking Free From Living Paycheck to Paycheck

I take it you want to quit paying to pay? Your objectives are to accumulate wealth, manage your finances, and achieve financial independence. You can achieve success if you put in the required effort, discipline, and dedication, even though it won't happen right now. Mostly, we require fresh concepts. Instead of fostering uncertainty, create possibilities. By acting and making wise choices, you can take control of your financial condition.

A budget that is made and adhered to is one of the most crucial steps toward financial independence. You can see where your money is going and identify areas where you may save by keeping track of your income and expenses. This will assist you with budgeting, money management, and debt avoidance. It's critical to control and minimize debt. Your money can be depleted and your development impeded by credit card debt and other significant financial responsibilities. Make a strategy to pay off your debts in a methodical manner, concentrating first on high-interest loans.You have a long time to save money. Create an emergency fund to assist cover unforeseen costs and steer clear of credit card use during hard times. Aim for three to six months of accumulation; transfer the remaining amount for your living expenditures to a readily available account. Make long-term investment and savings plans, such as emergency funds. Invest the tax savings in an IRA or 401(k) retirement account to help you save for the future. Investing in a diversified portfolio will minimize risk and increase long-term rewards.Increasing your income is a terrific method to progress toward independence, along with saving and investing.

Seek outside projects, pursue career growth chances, and never stop acquiring new skills if you want to remain competitive in the work market. Remember to be grateful for all of your victories along the way as you continue on your financial journey. Any financial accomplishment, whether it's debt repayment, savings growth, or goal completion, should be acknowledged and celebrated. Consider the good life, the noble life you aspire to, to keep yourself inspired and appreciative of your accomplishments.To sum up, you may stop paying to pay, but it will require time, effort, and the proper approach. Accept advice, set up a budget, pay off debt, save and invest sensibly, boost your income, and acknowledge and be proud of your accomplishments. Farewell on your journey to financial empowerment, and may your future be filled with prosperity, security, and abundance.

If you just finished reading this book your feedback is invaluable! If you found this guide helpful on your journey to financial independence and wealth management, please consider leaving a review on Amazon. Your review will not only help others discover the guide but also provide valuable insights for future readers. Thank you for your support!